valor total (Ful valiano)

FULL
VALUE

FULL VALUE

Proven Methods to Price & Sell Your Home for Maximum Profit

JACK RICHARDS

GREENLEAF
BOOK GROUP PRESS

Published by Greenleaf Book Group Press
Austin, Texas
www.gbgpress.com

Distributed by Greenleaf Book Group

For ordering information or special discounts for bulk purchases, please contact Greenleaf Book Group at PO Box 91869, Austin, TX 78709, 512.891.6100.

Design and composition by Greenleaf Book Group
Cover design by Greenleaf Book Group
Photographs on page 106 courtesy of Trey Thomas Photography

Publisher's Cataloging-in-Publication data is available.

Print ISBN: 978-1-62634-684-0

eBook ISBN: 978-1-62634-685-7

Part of the Tree Neutral® program, which offsets the number of trees consumed in the production and printing of this book by taking proactive steps, such as planting trees in direct proportion to the number of trees used: www.treeneutral.com

Printed in the United States of America on acid-free paper

20 21 22 23 24 25   10 9 8 7 6 5 4 3 2 1

First Edition

To my wife, Kristen, for without her continuous and unwavering support and encouragement this book would have never been completed.

"It's interesting. In our industry, you could write a book about someone whose best practices are allowing them to compete in a unique and advantageous way, and yet most of the industry would pretty much ignore that and keep doing things the way they were."

—**JEFF LUHNOW,** general manager of the Houston Astros, 2017 Major League Baseball World Series Champions

CONTENTS

xi . . . . Preface: Do Best Practices Exist in Real Estate?

1 . . . . Introduction: The Power of Data

11 . . . Part 1: Valuing Your Home

13 . . . . . . Chapter 1: How Home Value Is Determined

25 . . . . . . Chapter 2: Factors That Affect Home Value

41 . . . . . . Chapter 3: Finding Value

53 . . . Part 2: Preparing for the Sale

55 . . . . . . Chapter 4: First Impressions: Curb Appeal

63 . . . . . . Chapter 5: I Could Live Here

75 . . . Part 3: Marketing Your Home

77 . . . . . . Chapter 6: The Buyer's Perspective

91 . . . . . . Chapter 7: Setting the List Price

101 . . . . . Chapter 8: Developing an Effective Listing

117 . . . . . Chapter 9: Timing: When to Market

123 . . . . . Chapter 10: Selecting a Good Agent

133 . . Part 4: Closing the Deal

135 . . . . . Chapter 11: Negotiation

157 . . . . . Chapter 12: From Contract to Close

161 . . Conclusion: For Full Value

165 . . Acknowledgments

167 . . Appendix: Doing Your Own Due Diligence—A Home Seller Self-Assessment

183 . . Notes

191 . . Index

201 . . About the Author

DO BEST PRACTICES EXIST IN REAL ESTATE?

Every year millions of homes are bought and sold in the United States. Each sale is one of the largest financial transactions the buyer or seller will make in their lifetimes. Despite the size and impact of these transactions, few home sellers actually sell their homes in a way to maximize their profits. Fortunately, home sellers today are able to take advantage of insights generated through applied data analytics and advances in research in the academic fields of economics, psychology, and anthropology. These insights, proven through research, outline a clear and practical approach for home sellers to sell their homes for 5 percent or even 10 percent more than what would be possible without taking these actions.

My professional background is in strategy consulting. For years I have advised executives of global corporations on how to effectively grow their companies, optimize their operations, and make strategic decisions. No matter what question I was asked, my basic approach to answering the overall question was simple: Break down the complex problem into simpler and more easily answerable sub-questions and then use data to answer each of the sub-questions. These answers would then inform the answer to the overall question, and when the process was complete, I was able to confidently provide executives with comprehensive recommendations supported by data-backed insights.

Furthermore, I have spent much of my professional career working in process-based industries ranging from mining to manufacturing to professional services operations. A key to success in these industries is to establish stable, repeatable processes and then improve those processes with innovations and other process changes. Many of these organizations had similar operational processes in different locations. These companies, like every company, are challenged by operational performance differences. Different teams can be given the exact same equipment, but the performance of the teams can vary across all levels. The only differences between product sites are culture and leadership. One tool that can minimize the performance gap between high-performing teams and underperforming ones is to identify, document, and share best practices. These best practices can be as minor as what direction parts face at one stage of a manufacturing line or as major as designing a completely new process to incorporate new technology, such as automated assembly and inspection.

It was with this perspective of logical problem structuring, application of data-based insights, and continual process improvement that I observed the process of buying and selling residential real estate. The differences in how homes can be sold and the potential to improve the home sale process became obvious with the purchase of a townhome in Raleigh, North Carolina.

For many years my wife, Kristen, and I lived in New York City. Like many working professionals, we valued our experience in New York but decided to relocate to a more suburban area. We chose to move to Raleigh as we had family and friends in the area, and with the vibrant, growing economy, both of us could work in fields similar to those we had in New York. As we planned our move south, we decided that rather than rent a place to live, we would purchase a home in the Raleigh area.

We started the home buying process in the typical way, first by determining the radius where we wanted to live and establishing the price range for what we were looking for. For our location and budget, much of what we found were townhomes, which we were excited about, coming from a small New York City apartment. Next, we set about finding a real estate agent to help us and selected one based on a recommendation from someone we knew in the area.

The agent took a day to drive us around Raleigh. We looked at several homes that we had found online or that the agent suggested and ended up finding a townhome that appealed to us. It was an end unit, recently built, and surrounded by trees and a small pond. It had three stories, all finished. The townhome checked all of the boxes we were looking for, so we decided to take a more in-depth look at the home. During this process, we found a few aspects which concerned us and which required further evaluation. The property was located in a floodplain and close to a creek that was infamous for regularly flooding. On the state-required property disclosure form, several questions were answered *No representation*, indicating either that the owners simply did not know the response or that there were issues with the property they did not want to reveal on the form.

Despite these concerns, we liked the location and layout of the house and decided to submit an offer for the home. The townhome had been on the market for about three months.

We initially made an offer for the property at 93.5 percent of the listing price to gauge the sellers' interest in a quick sale. The sellers rejected our initial offer and came back with a counteroffer at 99.8 percent of the listing price, nearly unchanged from their original asking price. After another round of back-and-forth with the sellers, we agreed on an offer to purchase the townhouse for 98.4 percent of the asking price, which was a typical discount to the list price in the market at that time. We went under contract and began the due diligence process to ensure the safety, soundness, and legality of the home.

We hired several experts to look at the house. A home inspector checked the building for potential structural or safety issues. To understand the flood risk, we had a surveyor measure the building elevation relative to expected flood levels. To verify property ownership, a real estate attorney checked the property title. Thankfully, there were no surprises, and we took possession of the townhome.

About a year and a half later, we decided to move to a new home in the area. We decided to sell the townhome and began the home sales process that July.

Again, we hired a real estate agent. After interviewing others, we chose our agent for his knowledge of the market and his approach to selling homes. At his recommendation, we prepared the house for sale. We decluttered the home, removing everything apart from the bare minimum we needed to live in the house. We removed our personal photos around the home. We cleaned everything completely from floor to ceiling, baseboards to blinds. We hired carpet cleaners to give the upper floor carpets a like-new feel. We touched up the paint where needed. And, for outside, we purchased a few small plants to place by the front entrance to create a welcoming first impression.

We completed the required property disclosure form in its entirety and created a binder containing information from when we purchased the property, including the flood zone elevation certificate, the home inspection, and receipts of the work completed, such as the water heater replacement, and other appliance warranty paperwork.

Our agent hired knowledgeable, professional photographers to take photos of the interior and exterior. He also developed an 80-word listing description highlighting key differentiators, such as the "beautiful" and "well-maintained" home's "open floor plan" and "crown molding." After looking at comparable homes in the area and balancing those prices with our desire to sell quickly, we decided to list the home for a price over 10 percent higher than our purchase price. We listed it on a Thursday in early July and conducted an open house two days later. Within four days of listing, we received multiple offers and accepted a favorable offer thousands of dollars over our asking price. In the end, we sold the townhouse at a price over 15 percent higher than the price we paid only 16 months earlier.

We were lucky to have the tailwind of a healthy market, but something we did allowed us to buy a home that was on the market for three months at under asking price and then turn around in a little over a year to sell it at a price above list and well above the average appreciation for the Raleigh market. We also sold our home more quickly than other similar homes in the neighborhood and at a price comparable to arguably nicer homes.

How did this happen? Could it happen again? And what lessons from this experience could be applied more broadly? It turns out that you can greatly increase the chances of selling your home quickly and above the market rate by following a handful of simple steps. This book will discuss the how and why for each step along the way.

WHY WRITE THIS BOOK?

From the perspective of a business professional, selling our townhome was a fascinating experience. I was amazed at how two different real estate professionals could sell the same property and have such contrasting outcomes. I could not figure out how one agent could have such a difficult time selling the townhome in Raleigh and how another could sell it with multiple offers above list price just a year and a half later. The market had not changed dramatically in that time, so there was clearly something in what the agents—or we as owners—did to help sell the townhome. It appeared as if there was a specific formula to selling houses faster and for higher profit, but what was it? And was there data to support the answer? Using my consulting frameworks, I refined these questions into one overall question: What are the "best practices" in selling a house and by how much should these best practices improve performance?

This book represents my attempt to answer these two linked questions.

From my corporate experience, I did not wholly trust anecdotes and the so-called tips readily available online or from real estate agents. Experience had taught me to listen to these tips but only as ideas, ideas that would have to be verified with data. So I looked into the data.

I reviewed thousands of pages of recent academic studies and numerous industry reports and then tested these insights with experienced real estate agents and other industry professionals to determine which actions consistently improve the outcome for the seller. All of the recommended actions in this book are well understood and recognized by effective agents. By understanding the theory and application of a small set of actions or best practices, I believe home sellers can realize 5 percent or even 10 percent more than similar homes that do not take the recommended actions. My hope is that each one of you can shorten the time it takes to sell your home and increase the price you're able to sell it for. In short, I hope you are able to sell your home for its *full* value.

WHO IS THIS BOOK FOR?

This book was written to help residential home sellers maximize the sales price of their home. When I discuss maximizing a home's sales price, I mean achieving the seller's optimal outcome, which can vary based on an individual's needs. For some, selling at the highest possible price is the best outcome; for others, the most important outcome is selling quickly. For most sellers, however, the optimal outcome is somewhere between these two extremes and is a balance of selling a home for a good price in a reasonably short amount of time. Any action that increases the sales price could also shorten the time to contract at a corresponding lower price point.

The goal of this book is to demonstrate how completing a number of relatively small actions can have a significant impact on the final sales price of a home. This knowledge will help homeowners to maximize their investment in their home, help real estate agents better advise their clients, and provide real estate investors with insights to increase the return on their investment.

For homeowners

Homeowners looking to sell will learn what actually matters to buyers. There is an overwhelming amount of information available to potential sellers. All sorts of vendors will want you to purchase their products and services, and each one will claim that purchasing their offering will help the resale value of your home.

Yes, you could spend $60,000 to completely remodel your kitchen, but this would be worth less than $40,000[1] to a buyer when selling your home. Technically, the value of your home would increase, but you would have spent more than you recouped. The same applies to replacing windows, remodeling a bathroom, adding a room to the house, and nearly every other major renovation project. Virtually no remodeling project returns the cost of the job when it comes to selling a house.

Knowing that most homeowners will not recoup their money spent on home renovations, I will cover the actions that do. Some, such as cleaning and decluttering a home, are old classics. The well-worn tropes actually work and have a tangible impact on how buyers perceive the house. Other actions, such as improving curb appeal, provide valuable insights that tend to be underemphasized when selling, because the true impact is generally not well understood by sellers. In the following chapters, I will cover what is important, what works, and where I recommend spending money to maximize the sales price of your home.

These recommendations are not glitzy. There will not be a TV show highlighting these findings. Nearly everything I recommend is routine, basic, and subtle. The purpose here is not to show off to the neighbors or follow the latest crazy trend. This book is laser-focused on helping you achieve results that maximize the sales price of your home.

These pages should help you understand what drives the value of residential homes, what buyers value, what actions you can take to help buyers want your home, and how to ensure your agent is working for you to maximize your sales price.

For real estate agents

For real estate agents, this book covers wide ground. The intent is to help you become more knowledgeable about home pricing and enable you to provide superior service to your clients. The foundational pricing content will allow you to translate how items in the local news such as changes in local employment, new home construction, and available inventory can impact an individual house's value. You will also better understand sources of value that may not be fully recognized or captured in CMAs, AVMs, or other home valuations. Finally, you will be provided a specific set of recommendations for you and your clients to implement. Many of these you already know and use today, while others may be new or at least more nuanced than your current practices. I want to help you serve your clients better and in the process help you grow your business.

I also understand your time is valuable, and I strongly believe the insights in these pages will help you sell your clients' homes at a higher price—an outcome in your best interest. To be more specific, let's run the numbers. We can start by calculating the difference in a commission using the example of a $392,000 home. If we assume the house sells for 100 percent of list and has a traditional commission of 6 percent, a 50/50 agent listing/selling agent split, and an 80 percent broker payout rate, then the pocketed difference for selling this house for 5 percent more is over $470.[2] This difference is additional income for simply working smarter, not harder. Your clients are happy with the higher price, and you benefit financially from every house you sell.

I believe the recommendations highlighted in this book are practical and meaningful, and I hope they will have a practical and meaningful impact on your business.

For real estate investors

For real estate investors, flippers, rehabbers, or anyone who buys residential properties with the intent to resell for profit, I want to help you ensure you buy and then sell at the best prices possible. The chapters on the economics of residential real estate will help you identify undervalued properties and avoid properties that could be difficult to sell at a profitable price. I will identify areas of value that may not be recognized by the seller or the seller's agent but that you can capitalize on. I also provide tips and techniques on how to prepare your homes for sale.

I also emphasize the importance of being a professional in the truest sense of the word. Professionals in other industries, such as music and sports, spend thousands of hours perfecting their craft and delivering a world-class product. With the insights in this book, I want to help you become the best professional in your area of real estate.

THE POWER OF DATA

Buying or selling a house is one of the largest financial transactions most people conduct in their lifetimes. These transactions are also emotional and rare. Buying a house requires extensive knowledge across subjects ranging from legal requirements and finances to construction, zoning, and environmental regulations. Most home buyers and sellers work with a team of experts throughout the course of a single transaction. But despite the magnitude of the purchase, little emphasis is placed on how to price and market the home with the expectation to maximize the outcome for the seller.

This lack of emphasis is not because it is not possible to differentiate a home in the market. Most sellers—and their agents—try to sell homes using a general, imprecise approach. Prices are set by gut instincts and personal preferences, not necessarily with insights proven by data. The selling process is established by what sellers feel like doing and maybe by what they did in a previous sale. For most sellers, OK is good enough. In today's world, however, just OK is becoming less acceptable. With the rise of the internet and easily available data on home sales prices, along with photos, floor plans, and even financial information, just OK should not be good enough for savvy house sellers. We need to use every edge available and take advantage of the growing body of knowledge to maximize a home's sales value and to do this by pairing the home you are selling with a buyer who is excited to have the opportunity to purchase that home.

We live in an increasingly data-rich world. Insights from this data can help us make decisions to improve outcomes including selling homes at a higher price than what would be possible selling the "normal" way.

DATA ANALYTICS

The use of data analytics is changing industries. Organizations are using data-based insights to change their approaches to how they compete and where they make investments. In major league sports, data analytics have changed how teams operate. Data-based insights in baseball have changed recruiting, pitching, and how teams prepare for each opposing batter. In basketball, data analytics have shown how the reward of taking three-point shots outweighs the risk. Insights like this, along with the talent to execute them, led the Golden State Warriors to successive National Basketball Association championships.[1]

The use of data analytics has also influenced the corporate world. Data-backed insights have led to organizations taking actions to improve outcomes. These insights have changed how businesses operate in nearly every industry. In mining, the use of better data has allowed mines to extract minerals by targeting where the best ore is found. In agriculture, farmers can increase crop yields through precision application of fertilizers, pesticides, and water, ensuring an exact amount is provided only where and when it is needed. Other companies use data analytics in their sales process to improve their lead generation, structure their sales force, and maximize how they sell to their customers.[2]

Mastering advanced pricing techniques is increasingly required for companies to stay competitive, so leading companies invest significant resources to understand how to optimize the pricing of their products using data-backed insights. These companies understand how small improvements in pricing can make a meaningful improvement to a company's profitability. Applying advanced analytics to a data set of product sales can show businesses the effects of using price adjustments, discounts, rebates, or other changes and can project those effects on sales and profitability in the future. Companies are increasingly making pricing changes in real time to adjust for varying demand. They have also figured out how to change different prices at the individual consumer level.

Like other markets, the residential real estate market is undergoing rapid change brought on by technological innovation. Data aggregators and information companies, such as Zillow, Trulia, and Redfin, are making home values more transparent and readily available to anyone. Homes for sale can be seen online and in great detail. Virtual home walkthroughs and 3-D models are now commonly available on major real estate websites. Thus, today's home buying process differs greatly from that of the past. Overall, home buyers are more informed about the home buying process and the inventory available in their local markets. This change represents an opportunity to sellers who understand this new system and who can adapt how they meet the needs of savvy home buyers.

Despite the prevalence of advanced technology and the transparency of publicly available pricing information, the specifics of pricing an individual home remain imprecise. Rarely do any two sources estimate the value of a house to be the same. If you ask 10 different appraisers, real estate agents, and automated computer models for the market value of a house, you will get 10 different answers, with a large range between the lowest and the highest estimates. Professional real estate agents often refrain from picking a single price; when asked, they usually recommend a sales price range. When working with home sellers, the agent then puts the onus on these sellers to set the specific listing price. Unfortunately, home sellers are often the least informed parties, and these sellers do not have a deep understanding of the implications of their choices.

The truth is that pricing a home is an imprecise process. And like any other imprecise process, the level of variability could be either a positive or a negative for the home seller, and this impact is magnified by the size of the total dollars involved. A small increase in a realized sales price can have a sizeable impact on a family's income. In 2017 the average home in the United States sold for approximately $392,000.[3] If sellers complete the basic actions we will cover, we could expect to sell their house for potentially an additional 5 percent. Calculating the difference shows us this small 5 percent increase would result in additional income of roughly $19,600 to the seller. Taking this one step further, the median household in the United States has an annual income of approximately $59,000.[4] The value of that additional $19,600 is like receiving a bonus worth four months of work. That's four months of work equivalent to the relatively small amount of additional investment and time to sell your home properly. In short, the investment is worth the reward.

Fortunately, the rise of data analytics is beginning to change how residential homes are bought and sold. In the same way that data has informed how baseball teams recruit players or the kind of shots basketball players should take, residential home sellers can take specific actions to sell their homes at a higher price. Each of these actions, when taken individually, may not have a large impact on the selling price of a home, but when added together, they become meaningful and can result in a sales price of 5 percent or even 10 percent over what would normally be expected without taking this set of actions.

A 5 percent to 10 percent improvement may not help a sports team win every game, but over the course of a season, it can lead to a championship. Similarly, not every house sold will benefit every time using the applied tools, as each sale takes place under different circumstances. The purpose of this book, however, is to put the odds of a successful sale in your favor.

In the following chapters, I share a number of actions that can increase the selling price of your home. I understand the reality, though: Most home sellers will not take action on every recommendation. The reasons will be varied. Some actions require a little effort; others require some cost. The supporting professionals on the selling team, such as agents or contractors, may not be knowl-edgeable about each action's impact. But following this advice will differentiate an extraordinary sale from the ordinary—worth that 5 percent to 10 percent sales price increase. To achieve a successful sale, you need to think of the buyer's perspective and what they are looking for as they search for their new home. The actions high-lighted in this book are focused on making the buying process a positive and energizing experience for the buyers, because it is these happy and interested buyers who will gladly give you the higher price for your home. Make them want to buy your home, and you will benefit from a higher price and a quicker sale.

Just as championship sports teams and successful global com-panies seek to maximize any advantage over their competition, the insights in this book can help you sell your house more quickly or at a higher price than would be possible using otherwise normal everyday methods. And remember: Increasing the sales price of your home by just a few percentage points can mean a large difference in the dollar amount you take home after a successful sale.

USING DATA TO CREATE VALUE

In broad terms, selling a house consists of three phases: (1) deciding to sell and selecting an agent, (2) preparing the house for sale, and (3) marketing, negotiating the offer, and closing the sale. According to the National Association of Realtors, 89 percent of US home sell-ers use the assistance of an agent to sell their home.[5] Most sellers choose an agent they know—usually a friend or family member, an agent they have worked with previously, or referrals from friends, family, or previous agents. The sales preparation phase entails digging out paperwork related to when the seller purchased the home, cleaning the house, doing minor repairs to fix obvious deficiencies, and perhaps refreshing the appearance of a few rooms. At the same time, the agent is preparing to market the home. The agent looks at the local market conditions and the differentiating factors of the house and then develops a likely selling price range, and they have the home photographed inside and out. The agent also completes the paperwork required to list the home on the multiple listing service (MLS). Finally, the house is actively listed on the MLS and is shown to potential buyers by their own agents. The seller's agent may decide to host an open house. Ideally, buyers submit one or more offers quickly, negotiations are limited, and the buyer and seller agree to a contract. Most buyers will complete a due diligence process, arrange financing, and progress to the point of closing, where the transaction is finalized and the property formally changes ownership.

Throughout this process most sellers and many agents do not understand how they are leaving value on the table. This value comes from what a buyer is willing to pay for the home. The home seller can create additional value when they are able to capture what economists call *utility*. Utility is essentially the usefulness of what is being exchanged. Estimating how much value a certain action will add to a house is complicated. Unlike most consumer products, residential homes sell rarely, and each home is unique in many ways. Consumer products such as milk or movie tickets regularly sell in high volumes. Optimizing profits for these items through pricing or additional sales can easily be tested using a variety of well-known techniques.

If a certain pricing strategy is ineffective or the service offering is not valued by the customer, then the selling company can change what is needed and continue to sell without risking their entire business. Product owners can conduct small-scale trials to see what is more effective. Unfortunately, individual home sellers do not have the luxury to test their product and pricing with focus groups and analytical insights. For a single home, sellers can only ask "what if" to understand if they could have sold their home for more or how much less they should have initially priced a home that failed to sell. Home sellers essentially have just one chance to get it right.

Fortunately for homeowners today, the availability of large data sets, advanced analytical techniques, and low-cost computation power allow us to learn which actions can truly make a difference in a realized price for home sellers. One method for understanding the total value of a home is to break down the unknown total value into its individual components and then add up the value of each component to get a sum of the parts. Using this approach has a number of challenges including understanding what each part of a home is worth, but this is a challenge academics and economists understand and have developed tools to address.

Two common analytical tools for understanding the magnitude of a particular attribute's impact on home prices are paired-data analysis and hedonic regression. Although we will not go into detail about these methods, understanding what they are, how they work at a high level, and what their limitations are will allow us to understand how a value is determined and will provide us with a level of confidence in the data insights as you move from research to application in selling your home for its maximum price.

As the name indicates, a paired-data analysis compares the sales price of a property with a specific feature to the sales price of a recently sold similar property that does not have the same feature. After adjusting for other characteristic differences between the paired sales, such as age, size, and condition, the difference in the sales prices attributed to the feature can be estimated. In one report, California-based appraiser Sandra Adomatis noted, "The reliability of the paired-data analysis is based on the quantity and quality of the pairs. In most appraisal reports, appraisers are fortunate to find one good pair to support an adjustment in the sales comparison approach. All pairs are not expected to result in the same number because the market is not perfect and market participants vary in the price premiums they may be willing to pay."[6] Paired-data analysis provides one level of insight into the value of certain home attributes.

An alternative method to a paired-data analysis is the hedonic regression. Commonly used in economics and specifically in real estate economics, hedonic regressions estimate revealed preferences for features as part of the whole price. The method usually uses a regression analysis and decomposes the value of an item into its constituent parts. Using a residential house as an example, hedonic regression results could show that 62 percent of the value of the home is due to the square footage, 20 percent to the number of bedrooms, and the remaining 18 percent to the remaining 10 other attributes analyzed. The quality of this analysis is based on both the data set used for the regression and the variables chosen to be studied.

Today, a third and somewhat different approach is increasingly common beyond the paired-data analysis and hedonic regression. Real estate information websites such as Zillow, Trulia, Redfin, and others have assembled massive databases of house sale information and are now able to run analyses on these large data sets to look for meaningful insights. As software becomes more powerful and data sets become larger, insights are now becoming available for the relationship between specific words of a listing description or the color of a dining room on the final sales price of a home. The results from this big-data approach may not necessarily show how one factor directly influences another, but they can show a relationship between two data points. Once a relationship is identified, we can then develop a perspective on what factors, such as room colors, could influence another factor such as sales price.

Each of these methods has one goal: to identify specific factors that influence home sale values. Each method has its benefits and its flaws; however, when one begins to bring each of the insights together into a single picture, clear themes emerge and provide evidence that certain actions do help houses sell at a higher price. Taken together, value for the homeowner is added through a combination of, first, what the house already is, has, and where it is located, and second, how it is presented as a product, and finally, how it is marketed. Sellers cannot cost-effectively do much to change the home and its location. Sellers can, however, greatly influence how the house is presented and how the house is marketed.

PART 1

VALUING YOUR HOME

As we begin discussing how to price a home, you need to first embrace a difficult concept for most home sellers: Your house is not a home. At least, for the purpose of selling your home for its fullest value, you must distance yourself from your personal connections to the house and remain focused on making the house an attractive product for a buyer. For homeowners who have lived in one house for decades, who raised a family there, who spent a significant percentage of their lifetime there, the building is more than just a product. It is the place they return to after being away. It represents comfort, laughter, and family. It is home. This is understandable. But when you are preparing to sell your home, it becomes a product to be sold. To sell a house for full value, you need to develop this objective perspective and look to the needs of future owners, not share the history of the home at this point.

And, like with any product, we must highlight the selling points of the home, show how it is different from other products on the market, and help buyers discover how much they want to buy that house. We can use that information to determine its market value, but to do that, we must understand the market. We'll first discuss how value is determined for a residential property, then what factors might lead to fluctuations in that value. We will then look at sources of potential value frequently ignored by industry professionals.

HOW HOME VALUE
IS DETERMINED

All houses have a certain level of pricing uncertainty around a central point. This uncertainty creates a zone of potential prices, and any price in that zone would be considered within expectations for buyers. This zone of price uncertainty usually ranges between 5 percent and 10 percent of the value of the home, and this figure is based broadly on the price variability seen across most residential real estate markets in the United States. We also increasingly know the value of the elements that comprise a home's total value. By understanding how home prices fall into a range, that the range of acceptable pricing is somewhat wide, and which elements contribute to a home's value, we can then set a price in the zone of uncertainty favorable toward the seller. Actually selling a home for this favorable price can be accomplished by creating a better product for the buyer and by marketing this product to effectively maximize buyer interest.

Most studies evaluating home values identify factors that can influence the price of a home by 1 percent, 2 percent, or even 5 percent or 10 percent. We have all seen similar anecdotes: Do thing A and increase the value of your home by X percent; do thing B and you will increase the value by Y percent. If you individually added every insight together, you could find factors that total up to 40 percent of a selling price. This is where some common sense must come into play. It is highly unlikely that asking 40 percent over a typical asking price would result in a sale, much less a quick one. Individual studies tend to focus on one or two key attributes and deemphasize many others. While it's good to understand the relative magnitude and direction in which certain factors can influence price, I consider a total of 5 percent or 10 percent to be the upper bound in pushing the pricing limit. On a $392,000 home, adding 5 percent adds $19,600 to the price and makes the new price $411,600. Adding 10 percent adds $39,200 and would set the price at $431,200. I believe these are realistic ranges to target. Adding 30 percent to a $392,000 home and asking $509,600 would be excessive and rejected by most buyers.

Overpricing a home is a major risk for sellers and will result in a slow sale, no sale, or significant price reductions. Houses with multiple price reductions or sitting on the market for a long time raise questions for buyers and are likely to sell at a discount to the original expected selling price and lower than if the home were priced correctly at the start of the listing process. The challenge for everyone involved in selling a house is to find the right balance of capturing the true value of the home while not overpricing a house so that it does

Cómo conseguir el precio más porsible a la propiedad

not sell or sells at a lower price than would be possible. The first step to selling a house for 5 percent to 10 percent more than the expected selling price is to determine the expected selling price. *ojo*

Real estate agents begin the process of pricing a home by identifying similar homes that are comparable to the house being evaluated or sold; these are what are known as comparables or, as the professionals say, comps. Agents identify comps by looking for similar homes that have sold recently—for example, in the last three or six months—and have a location and features similar to the house being sold. Homes in the same neighborhoods tend to have similar characteristics of size, age, upkeep, and design, and these work well as comps for pricing purposes. Ideally, agents would find three or four usable comps for comparison. To estimate the expected selling price of a certain home, adjustments are made to the sales price of each comp for differences in the home compared with the target home. These adjustments account for differences in the number of bedrooms and bathrooms, the total square footage, whether the house has a fence, the presence of a newly remodeled kitchen, and any other considerable differences. These adjusted comps are then averaged in some way, usually weighted toward the most relevant comp, to develop a range of probable selling prices and within that range a single most likely selling price point.

AUTOMATED VALUATION MODELS

Before we dive deeper into understanding how to establish home prices, we should discuss the growing influence of automated valuation models (AVMs). The prevalence of computing power and large *regression*

Bureau hedonic regress

data sets permeates society today, and the residential real estate market is certainly not immune to the effects of technological advances.

For most sellers, AVMs are the first place people look to estimate the value of their house. Popular AVMs are those used by Zillow, Trulia, Redfin, and Chase Bank. These models are useful as a starting point for sellers but carry the risk of the model-generated home values being significantly different from the true market price of a specific home. While these models continue to improve, the error ranges can be substantial, and sellers who use this information should be sure to understand the limitations of these figures. Despite the flaws inherent in these models, the estimated prices are readily available to interested buyers and sellers who do use these values to set price expectations for a purchase or sale.

Understanding how these numbers are developed, though, can help you in effectively using these figures when selling a home. Most AVMs are constructed in a similar fashion, and the process for generating a price estimate is generally similar. To estimate the value of a specific home, an AVM identifies recent comparable sales within a close geography. These models look at individual home data, such as square footage, the number of bedrooms and baths, the year constructed, and other information to determine which recent sales are the most comparable. These models pull data from publicly available county-level databases and match with additional data available on local MLS sites (multiple listing service, used by real estate brokers to estimate house values). The models then determine the value of property components using a data analytics method, likely a hedonic regression. Alternatively, the models incorporate building cost estimates into their weighted formulas. These estimated home values are then calibrated to match actual sales. Finally, the models look at national, regional, and local pricing trends to adjust their estimated home values to reflect the market appreciation.[1]

AVMs do a heroic job at estimating home values and have come a long way since their inception, but they can still fall short in accuracy. In a widely reported transaction, former Zillow CEO Spencer Rascoff sold his Seattle home for $1.1 million or about 40 percent less than its Zestimate of $1.75 million at the time.[2] In comments to the media, Rascoff reiterated that these estimates are simply "good starting points"[3] and not a true pricing estimate.

Every AVM has limitations. On its website, Zillow clearly states that its median error rate nationally is 1.9 percent for on-market homes and 7.7 percent for homes not being sold, which means the Zestimates for half of all off-market homes are within 7.7 percent of the selling price, and half are off by more than 7.7 percent.[4] Trulia also provides updated data on the accuracy of its Trulia Estimate. As of mid-2018, Trulia's median error was 5.3 percent. Nationally, 48 percent of its estimates were within 5 percent of the sales price, and 68 percent were within 10 percent of the sales price.[5] Said differently, nearly one-third of Trulia's estimates were off of the sales price by more than 10 percent. A similar level of accuracy is common across all AVMs. Each model can be off by 5 percent or more, and it would be considered luck if they estimated any given price precisely. AVMs cannot routinely predict prices accurate to within a few percentage points, emphasizing the imprecision of sales prices and the opportunity for savvy sellers to sell at the top end of this zone of pricing.

Although AVMs are not accurate enough for setting a listing price, these models do provide a reasonable valuation starting point, especially when you average the outputs of multiple models, and the accuracy of these models continues to improve every year. Nevertheless, it is still best to supplement the use of AVMs with a local expert who can account for variables such as interior condition to develop a more accurate price range for a specific house in a specific market.

establiciendo la linea de base
(establàusin de base Ueseline) Ueslain)

ESTABLISHING THE BASELINE

The first step to selling a house for 5 percent to 10 percent more than the expected selling price is to know the expected selling price. This value establishes the baseline price from which we can work to sell for a higher price. The expected selling price can be developed using several methods. One method is to use an AVM estimate or, more preferably, an average of different AVM estimates to calculate a single price point. Alternatively, a knowledgeable real estate professional such as an agent or an appraiser could develop a point estimate using the comparable method. A third approach is to combine estimates from both AVMs and real estate professionals to establish a single expected selling price.

In this third approach, we can use the values of adjusted comparables (comparable homes whose prices have been adjusted in a way to account for the differences between the comp and the home being sold) and AVM estimates to arrive at a price range and expected selling price. The process of finding and adjusting for comps usually generates three or four relevant comparables, and home sellers can refer to their favorite AVMs for their price estimates. Taken together, these data points will paint a picture of what the likely selling price of the home will be as the estimated comparable price points tend to cluster around a single point with the differences from this point creating a range. Using our $392,000 home example, a comparables analysis or AVM output might show price estimates of our house to be something like this:

- Comparable 1: $380,000
- Comparable 2: $397,000
- Comparable 3: $390,000
- Comparable 4: $388,000
- AVM 1: $394,560
- AVM 2: $408,000
- AVM 3: $386,000

Using our example above, the lowest value estimate in our list of seven prices is Comparable 1 at $380,000, and the highest price estimate is AVM 2 at $408,000. If we are lucky, the range will be tight and within 2 percent to 3 percent in either direction. For our $392,000 home, this would be plus or minus roughly $8,000–$12,000. More likely is the broader range of 5 percent to 10 percent. In our example above, Comparable 1 is about 3 percent below our $392,000 estimate, and AMV 2 is about 4 percent higher than our $392,000 average. Without knowing the value of our house is $392,000, we would feel confident that it was worth between $380,000 and $408,000. It is highly probable that a sales price will occur within this range (see Figure 1.1).

Figure 1.1. *Range of likely sales prices*

Within this range is the point at which the house is most likely to sell, the expected selling price. This price will usually be somewhere toward the middle of the range or at a point where the price estimates cluster. In our example in Figure 1.1, the seven different price estimates average out to $392,000.[6] This single point is our best estimate of the expected selling price of a home selling under normal circumstances (see Figure 1.2).

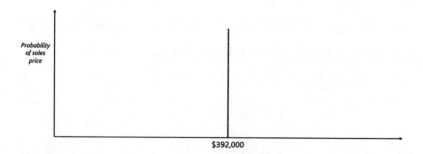

Figure 1.2. *Single point price estimate*

Numerous factors can affect the range of sales prices in an area. Different people and situations can lead to different optimal outcomes, and money may not be the main driver. A seller looking for a quicker sale may value time over money and may choose to sell at a lower price if the sale can close faster. Price is only one variable in the deal to sell a house. Although the likely price may be $392,000, using our example, an owner looking for a quick cash sale may be very happy selling for $380,000. Alternatively, a buyer finding the perfect home with a very flexible move-in date could be willing to pay a higher cash price for the convenience of closing on their schedule. Using our example, this would be the buyer who offers $408,000 for the house. In between $380,000 and $408,000 are numerous other possibilities that could be either above or below our probable selling price of $392,000 shown in Figure 1.3.

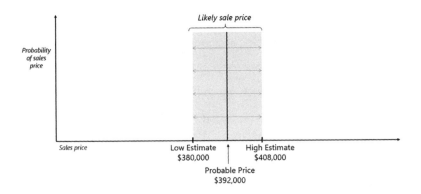

Figure 1.3. *Range of likely selling prices and the probable price*

Complicating matters further are sales that include more or less than the standard set of rights that come with property transactions in the United States. Some sales may exclude or separately sell the

mineral and gas rights for a property. Some may include the trac-
tor lawnmower that the downsizing family will no longer need as
they transition from a farmhouse to a suburban apartment. Cash-
constrained buyers may highly value a seller's contribution to closing costs. Again, the concept of a pricing range remains valid and the
uncertainty considered when establishing the baseline price.

Additionally, one-off events can create extreme outliers in pricing. At the extreme low end of the pricing range, a quick, low-price
sale may be required for personal reasons. An owner may be highly
motivated to sell for reasons such as a job change, divorce, or death.
When looking at a sales price range, these factors would lead to a sales
price that is artificially low. The seller does not benefit as much, but
they realize their economic utility otherwise (through a quick sale).
Institutional sellers, such as banks, are frequently willing to take a
lower price to sell a property faster.

At the other extreme, although less common than the quick sellers,
there may be buyers willing to pay significantly more for a certain property. A buyer may strongly desire the property because of the family living next door, the property being a childhood home, an unusually large
number of bedrooms for an unusually large family, or a house being
previously owned by a favorite celebrity. For these buyers, adjacent
houses could be nicer or a better value or could in many other ways be
considered superior, but it is that specific home that the buyer is interested in purchasing. They will pay a premium for that specific house. I
was impressed by one real estate agent who reached out to a colleague
expressing interest in purchasing their home on behalf of a client
who wanted a specific floor layout they could not find on the market.

This specific sort of demand tends to generate prices higher than the expected sales price because of the rare circumstances.

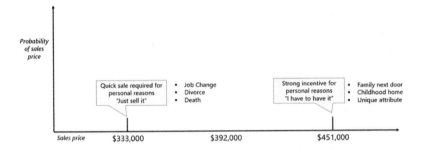

Figure 1.4. *Outlier price scenarios*

When the range of prices and the likelihood of selling at those prices are compiled, you would expect to see a distribution similar to a bell curve. The probability of selling at a certain price is highest at its expected sales price, but it is possible—although less probable—to sell at a price at the extremes. It is this range of uncertainty that allows us the potential to sell a home for more than the expected asking price.

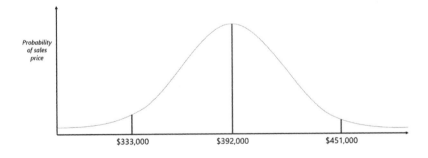

Figure 1.5. *Distribution of potential selling prices*

This distribution can be seen in real-world data. Analysts at the web-site Priceonomics asked a similar question.[7] Using a data set containing sales prices and list prices across San Francisco in 2014, the researchers plotted the range of discounts or premiums of the sales prices. They found a distribution that looked similar to a normal distribution curve, with most houses selling within 10 percent of the list price. Given the strong market in San Francisco at the time of the study, the distribution curve tended to shift more toward the positive side, because more houses sold at more than 10 percent above their list prices and fewer homes sold at less than 10 percent of the list price than one would normally expect. And as is normal with most large sets of data, the distribution contained outliers in both directions, with some homes selling at 25 percent below list price and others at a 40 percent or 50 percent premium to the list price. The majority of homes, though, sold in a relatively narrow range around the list price.

House prices are variable and uncertain. Financial and nonfinancial factors influence the final price. All of these factors allow us to take advantage of pricing ambiguity and offer an attractive house product to the market with the confidence that we can shift our pricing probabilities upward and realize an increased sales price of 5 percent or even 10 percent more.

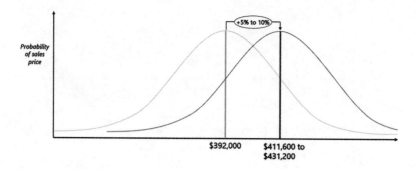

Figure 1.6. Shifted probable sales price of 5 percent to 10 percent

FACTORS THAT AFFECT HOME VALUE

"Location. Location. Location." These words are regularly heard when discussing real estate. But why does a property's location matter? Because developed real estate has two components that provide value. The first component is the unmovable land that establishes location. Land provides both the literal and figurative foundation for a home's value. The second component is what is known as improvements and includes constructed items such as buildings, utilities, and driveways. These two components share an address but, from an economic perspective, have completely different characteristics. At its most obvious, land is what makes a property appreciate. Improvements require continual investment to maintain value and without a level of continual investment in maintenance and upgrades will lose value. Over the past decades in the United States, property values have generally appreciated over the long term, and this is a function of the value of the land component, not the improvements. This difference between land and improvements is crucial to our understanding of how to value a home. Simply put, the key to real estate understanding is *land appreciates; buildings depreciate.*

Let's take an example of a typical house in the Chapel Hill, North Carolina, area. Chapel Hill is a quintessential university town, home to the University of North Carolina's flagship campus. A typical house for the area would measure about 2,000 square feet, with three bedrooms, three bathrooms, and a two-car garage on a lot of approximately 0.20 acres. This house, in a typical subdivision, would have sold for roughly $170,000 in 1991 and resold for, say, $209,000 in 1999 for an increase in value at a rate of roughly 2.4 percent annually. This same home would have sold again in 2005 for $265,000 and then again in 2018 for $365,000. Since it was initially constructed, the building itself would have been only modestly improved, with a remodeled kitchen, updated paint, and well-maintained flooring but no other major upgrades or additions. Nevertheless, the value of the home would have doubled over the last 30 years.

In this example, the house itself did not contribute to this increased valuation; the land did. The homeowners had to invest a healthy amount of capital to maintain their home's value. They conducted routine maintenance of the home's interior and exterior. They probably had to replace their roof, their HVAC system, and their water heater at least once. They spent thousands or tens of thousands of dollars to modernize their kitchen. Had the owners chosen to not maintain their home, the value of the property would be far less, but it would likely still be higher than the new price of the home in the 1990s, even with the lack of updates.

Most homeowners know that houses require investment to maintain value, but they may not know where to invest that money for their best financial returns. An investment in new, upgraded flooring could maintain or even increase the value of a property. Installing a swimming pool, however, could lower the home's value, despite the investment in the property, because the burden of maintaining a pool and having less available yard space could be turnoffs for many buyers. The owner who installed the pool may have enjoyed many hours in and around the pool, but the same owner should also not assume that having a pool definitively makes the home more valuable than similar homes without a pool.

The concept that land appreciates and buildings depreciate is the foundation of understanding how homes are valued. We can build on this knowledge to develop our understanding of what actually makes the land component of a home appreciate and where we can invest our limited funds to make select improvements to a building to maximize the resale value. Combined, the influencing factors of land and improvements help us establish our range of estimated home prices and allows us to more precisely assign a selling price range to the property.

FORCES AFFECTING PROPERTY VALUES

Land value can be understood at three levels. The first level is the region where the land is located. Going one level deeper is the neighborhood, which has a meaningful impact on the property value. And, finally, the third level is the specific lot and house itself. Let's work through each level.

The region

One reasonable way to define a region is to think about how you would answer the question "Where are you from?" Few people answer the question by saying a neighborhood or by giving a specific street address. Nearly everyone responds by saying the name of the nearest large city or, if there are no large cities nearby, by saying some part of a state—that is, the region.

Each region has its own specific real estate market, and the dynamics affecting one region do not necessarily affect others. For example, identically constructed homes can have vastly different prices, depending on their respective regions. This difference in value can be understood by examining the factors that affect property value, such as demographics, proximity to people and activities, the physical attributes of the region, the local political climate, and the local economy.

Regional demographics inform who is a likely buyer for your home. A large average family size can mean that homes with more rooms will sell faster or for more; a younger or older population—people not living with children—will favor smaller homes. A region with a large aging population may mean increased value for homes with a downstairs master or near shopping relative to a three-story home located at the edge of town.

Physical attributes of a region, such as topography and climate, can also shape property values. Steep terrain can make home sites less desirable than a flatter site. A similar flat site on a floodplain, however, may have the opposite effect. A sunny climate, like in Southern California, may command higher home values than an area that experiences heavy snow or year-round cloud cover, like the Pacific Northwest.

Proximity to transportation, such as highways, airports, buses, and trains, is another regional factor influencing home prices.[1] Many home buyers consider a shorter commute more valuable than a longer one and will consider this value when purchasing a home.

Local, state, and national governments impact home prices through their policies on development and zoning. To highlight how local government policies can affect property values, a 2017 study by the CATO Institute concluded that "about 20% of the variation in metropolitan housing growth can be explained through density regulations" and that "anti-density regulation inflates prices in the face of demand shocks."[2]

Finally, economic forces, such as median income level, employment rates, and general economic growth influence property values.[3] Higher income and employment rates generally indicate higher home prices, as does economic growth.

These factors vary across regions and inform the levels of supply and demand for housing, as well as the associated baseline price for a home.

The neighborhood

Whereas the region informs the baseline price of a home, the neighborhood further influences that price. Three major factors shape neighborhood home values:

- *Schools.* The quality of local schools is often the single most important factor for buyers with children of school age.

- *Jobs.* Proximity to local employment is usually a high priority for most employment-age buyers.

- *Amenities.* Proximity to social and shopping centers is especially valued by younger buyers but plays an important role in pricing for all home buyers.

School quality and the impact on home prices has been the subject of many studies. Most of these studies associate higher quality schools with higher home prices. According to a 2016 ATTOM Data Solutions report, "homes in ZIP codes with at least one good elementary school have values about 77% higher than in ZIP codes without highly ranked schools close by."[4] The study considered "good" schools to be those that had overall test scores at least one-third above the state average, and the trend appeared to be valid over time. Furthermore, the study showed that homeowners living near good schools realized higher home value appreciation in terms of both total dollars and percentage increase.

Today, schools are graded by external organizations using data provided by the school or state. One researcher compared property values before and after Florida rolled out its statewide grading system in 1999. Florida began giving each school an explicit letter grade, from A to F. Given the local nature of schools and the granularity associated with home sales in each neighborhood, the study was able to estimate that an A-rated school in Gainesville added about $10,000 to the value of a home there versus a B school.[5]

Strong ratings lead to better community support, which in turn leads to better schools, a self-reinforcing cycle. According to the researcher, the difference between an A school and a B school could easily have been $50,000 on a $300,000 house 10 years later.[6] This cycle can be seen in locations across the country where the motto as it relates to real estate could be *a good school means less house for the same price.*

For working households without school-age children, the value of the commute may be of greater importance. As you would expect, the shorter the commute time, the higher the property value. Several studies have examined the relationship between property values and commute time. As one example, *The New York Times* looked at this relationship along its Metro-North commuter rail lines outside of New York City,[7] which travels north through Harlem and then north-east along the coast, eventually ending at New Haven, Connecticut. Along the way, the train passes through some of the nation's wealthiest areas, such as Greenwich and Darien, Connecticut.

Working with local appraiser Jonathan Miller, the study estimated the median home price per commuting minute at stops from Stamford to New Haven for areas where single-family homes were common. The study started its analysis after the first express stop at Stamford, located about 50 minutes from Grand Central Station, and evaluated stops farther into Connecticut with correspondingly longer commute times. The study found a consistent trend of homes with shorter commute times to Manhattan having higher median home prices per commuting minute. Homes in the Darien–Westport section of the line had median values in the $1.3 million to $1.4 million range, and a median price per commuting minute between $14,000 and $23,000. Farther away, the Southport and Fairfield stops, with 81-minute and 85-minute commute times, respectively, had median home prices per commuting minute of $7,000–$11,000. And for those at the end of the line, in the Stratford, Milford, and West Haven areas, a whopping 101- to 114-minute commute away from Grand Central Station, median home prices per commuting minute were a mere $1,600–$2,800. Despite the extremes along this route, the trend is clear: A shorter commute time increases the value of a home when compared with similar neighborhoods with longer commutes.

Looking at data in Seattle, Zillow found a similar relationship. For its 2018 analysis,[8] Zillow partnered with location platform company HERE Technologies. Together, the companies estimated peak commute time to downtown Seattle from every home in the Seattle area and matched those homes with Zillow's data on home size and house value (its Zestimate) or estimated rent. They then grouped homes into 20-minute commute bands (0–20 minutes, 20–40 minutes, 40–60 minutes, and more than 60 minutes) and looked at the characteristics of homes in each band.

The results provided another data point for valuing commute length. Zillow estimated that "the value of a typical Seattle metro home that is a 15-minute commute from the city center is $962,000, compared to $632,000 for the same home located a 40-minute commute away."[9] Said differently, a typical Seattle metro home with a

15-minute commute is valued at over 50 percent more than a similar home with a 40-minute commute. Additionally, since urban centers tend to be denser than other regions, the price per square foot closer to downtown would be expected to be higher, and the data support this. For both car and public transit commutes in Seattle, homes with peak commute times under 20 minutes cost 40 percent more per square foot than a typical home with a 20–40-minute commute.[10]

Finally, the ability to walk from a home to a restaurant or grocery store is valued by home buyers, and this desirability is reflected in home prices. Interestingly, the value of a walkable neighborhood is merely a step back to a historical norm. Before the advent of cars, neighborhoods tended to be compact and laid out in a network or a grid for quick access to town amenities. Most necessities would have been within a 10-minute walk, and this 10-minute walk radius would shape how neighborhoods were developed.[11] The rise of cul-de-sac neighborhoods of more recent decades eliminated much of the neighborhood connectedness to provide residents with quiet streets. Home buyers are increasingly seeing the value of being connected, and the value of a walkable neighborhood is increasing.

Walk Score, a private company, has attempted to quantify the walkability of a home. They have developed an algorithm that gives homes a score from 0 to 100 based on how close various amenities such as grocery stores, coffee shops, and other routine destinations are to the house.[12] Amenities within a five-minute walk, or 0.25 miles away, are given maximum points, and the number of points for an amenity decreases until the amenity is 30 minutes away and no points are given. A walk score of 90–100 is considered a walker's paradise, as daily errands do not require a car. At the other end of the spectrum, a score of 0–24 is considered car dependent because almost all errands require a car. Higher walk scores are associated with higher home values. A Zillow analysis estimated that a 15-point increase in walk score increased a home value by 6 percent to 24 percent. This number is closely tied to specific urban areas, with the high end of the range seen in large cities like Chicago.[13]

In another analysis, real estate brokerage Redfin observed the increasing value of a one-point increase in walk score. Redfin looked at the sales prices and walk score data of more than a million homes sold between January 2014 and April 2016 in 14 major metro areas. As their walk scores increased, so did the expected premium. As an example, Redfin found that increasing a home's walk score from 19 to 20 increased the sales price of the home by $181. An increase from 59 to 60 points provided a premium of $3,744. And increasing the walk score with a respectable 79 points by just one point to 80 added more than $7,000 of value.[14] Due to the increased value placed on walkability by today's home buyers, new housing developments are increasingly incorporating these concepts into their designs, and older developments and areas with high walkability are seeing increased home values compared with more disconnected areas.

The specific lot and house

We know that each house is unique, and this attribute is most apparent at the specific house and lot level. Property details, such as house size and lot location in a neighborhood, can greatly influence home values.

Across all products, tastes and preferences change over time. This is no different in the residential housing market. In the 1920s, the average size of a house was 1,048 square feet. By 1990, this average house size had nearly doubled, to 2,080.[15] This trend continues today, with ever-larger homes preferred by buyers. This preference for larger home sizes has implications for home sellers if they are marketing an older home that is smaller than today's preferences. These sellers would generally expect to sell at a lower square footage price, because fewer buyers would be interested in the smaller home if larger options were available on the market.

The effects of lot size and shape on property values are a bit more complicated. Buyers commonly hear that corner lots are worth a premium or that cul-de-sac lots are worth more than other lots. New home builders often charge a premium for these favorable lots. The data on the impact of lot premiums on resale properties, however, appears inconclusive. A 2014 study by a researcher at Duke University examined property values in Durham, North Carolina's Hope Valley neighborhood. The study looked at the value of homes on corner lots relative to those not on corner lots. The resulting analysis found neither a clear premium nor a discount for homes on a corner.[16] Muddying the truth are anecdotal arguments, which support both sides of a counterargument; for example, corner homes have increased crime because they are visible or corner homes have lower crime because the visibility deters criminal activity. For the purposes of selling a home for full value, we will make the call that corner lots are not intrinsically more valuable than other lots.

In a similar manner to corner lots, cul-de-sac lots also have the reputation of being more attractive to a set of buyers because of both the perception and the reality of increased vehicle safety and lower crime. A 1990 study looking at home values in Halifax, Nova Scotia, determined that cul-de-sac lots were valued up to 29 percent higher than comparable homes on a grid layout.[17] Admittedly, this finding is decades old and the trends are changing toward more connected neighborhoods such as those with high walkability, but some data do show a premium for cul-de-sac lots.

Altogether, the value of the home is highly influenced by factors related to the region, the neighborhood, and the specific lot and house. These factors do not remain the same over time. Regional economies cycle through times of prosperity and decline, population demographics evolve, and new developments occur. Neighborhoods can see new schools built or experience a change in population. And home styles go out of fashion. The impact of these attributes can increase or decrease the value of a home. Real estate investors are keenly attuned to these factors, because the future return on their investments can be significantly improved if their properties appreciate within a rising market.

APPRAISERS

Any discussion of home values would be incomplete without including the role of appraisers. An appraiser can affect the sales price of a home if they believe a buyer is paying too much for a purchase and if the lending bank, using the appraiser's assessment, then rejects the buyer's loan amount. Appraisal contingencies are a common feature in many purchase contracts and allow home buyers to back out of a contract if the house appraises below a defined amount. With this level of influence on a home sale, it is worth understanding how appraisers develop their estimates, the accuracy of their assessments, and the implications for setting an initial asking price well above similar homes.

An appraiser's job is to validate and confirm the approximate value of the house for sale, usually at the request of a bank or other financial lender. If the appraiser agrees that the contracted price for a home is equal to or lower than the value of the home, the financing bank will have confidence in providing the loan. If the appraiser estimates the home's value as significantly lower than the sales price, the transaction can then get more complicated and may require either a reduction in price or an increase in down payment to lower the bank's associated risk.

The role of appraisers has changed since the real estate collapse of the Great Recession of 2008. Federal requirements have streamlined the individual mortgage purchasing process, and the appraisal process has become more standardized—and more objective—across the United States. Today, appraisers must follow detailed guidelines for any federally backed mortgage, and the end report appraisers develop has been increasingly standardized. Although the process and results may be more standardized, the accuracy of appraisals has not increased. Appraising is as much art as science, and appraisers are likely to be as biased as any human whose job requires creating, selecting, and interpreting information.

At the start of a home purchase appraisal,[18] the appraiser is given a package of information, which includes a copy of the sales contract, complete with contract terms and the contract price. Appraisers know the sales price of a property at the start of the process, and this knowledge influences their appraisal.

Appraisers tend to fall prey to a common psychological trap called *confirmation bias*, the tendency to interpret information in a way that confirms one's existing beliefs or theories. With ambiguous evidence, people tend to find information that supports their existing position. For appraisers, this means they look for information to confirm the sales prices of the homes they are appraising.

Fannie Mae, the nation's largest secondary mortgage purchaser, completed a study in 2016 looking at this exact dynamic. It compared the appraised value to the purchase price for 17 million home loans that it had guaranteed between 1992 and 2015. Across this pool, Fannie Mae discovered that more than 64 percent of the appraisals came in above the transaction price.[19] Another 32 percent of the appraisals came in *exactly* at the transaction price. Less than 4 percent of the appraisals were below the purchase price. Having more than 96 percent of homes appraised at or above the sales price would indicate that either the residential real estate market is highly efficient and homes sell at exactly their value or that the appraisers show bias in their work.

To test for this bias, Fannie Mae looked at situations where a house was appraised twice in a short period, usually once before a sale to help value the house and then again after it was sold for the buyer's financing. In these situations, the first appraisal did not have the bias of an existing contract price, whereas the second appraisal did know the purchase price for the home. Unsurprisingly, the confirmation bias could be seen influencing the second appraisals.

In these second appraisals, the appraisers selected different comparables and comparables that tended to have sold for higher prices, on average, than the comparables selected for the first appraisal. The appraisers were also more positive in their adjustments in these second appraisals. Finally, when the appraisers averaged the comparables, they weighted more heavily those that would result in an appraisal at or above the contract price. Fannie Mae found out that, on average, the second appraisals, where the appraisers knew the contract price, were 4.2 percent higher than the initial appraisals. The study adjusted for any market movements in the short time between the appraisals, so the insights were clear: The appraisers were biased toward a contracted sales price.[20]

For Fannie Mae, this analysis raised questions on how best to control for these biases to obtain the most accurate valuation possible. It observed that there has been less bias since the postrecession process reforms were implemented, but a significant amount of appraiser bias remains.

For home sellers, this degree of error shows the fallibility of appraiser estimates. With the 4.2 percent error range identified by Fannie Mae, a $200,000 value estimate could be off by $8,400. For a $500,000 home, the appraisal could be off by $21,000 in either direction. And for a $750,000 home, the appraisal could be off by more than $31,500!

Knowing that there could be at least a 4 percent uncertainty in an estimate from an appraiser—an expert whose profession it is to determine home values—provides us further confidence that selling for 5 percent over comparable prices is not at all unreasonable. We need to know how appraisers do their job, but we should not lower our potential selling price out of fear of a low appraisal. Selling a home for 5 percent to 10 percent more is possible if the home is properly prepared for sale and marketed so the right buyer finds the home and is excited at the opportunity to purchase the home.

KNOW WHERE YOUR HOME'S VALUE COMES FROM

We started this chapter by walking through the major factors that influence a home's value at the regional, neighborhood, and specific house levels. These factors help explain why a house in one part of the country would sell at a price several times higher than a similar house in a different city. Each of these factors is generally beyond your control when you sell a house, but understanding these factors is crucial to knowing how to value your home.

When it comes to estimating specific house prices, there is no perfect answer. Real estate agents, computer models, and other professional valuations will help you determine a reasonable market price for your home, but these only get you close. It is up to you as a seller to determine the likely range of selling prices for the home. The broad neighborhood market sets the range of prices, but once the range is identified, you can take actions to ensure your home sells at its high end.

FINDING VALUE

Turn on cable TV at any time of the day, and you will find multiple shows on home improvement, buying real estate, renovating or flipping homes, or selling luxury homes. There is no lack of information on ideas for home improvements, and the abundance of information can be overwhelming. Frequent advice on how to improve a home includes these standards:

- "Replace your old windows."
- "Update your master bath."
- "Renovate your kitchen with stainless steel appliances and granite countertops."
- "Finish the attic." (Or the basement or even the garage)
- "Tear down nonstructural walls to create an open floor plan."
- "Make your home 'smart.'"

One common element across these recommendations is that each one involves significant costs. Yes, doing each of these jobs will probably increase the value of the home, but the increase in value is less than the cost of the improvements in nearly every case. You are not creating value if the cost of your investment does not pay off in additional value many times over. To create value, you must be laser-focused on the buyer's experience and target improvements only if they make a tangible impact on how the buyer perceives the home.

Renovating everything in the home is nice and could provide the sellers with some joy, but from a value perspective, you have to ask yourself, "Does the payback on the investment justify making the improvement?" The short answer is no. In most cases, the payback is less than the cost of the investment and does not justify the spending on the upgrade. According to the well-regarded *Remodeling* magazine's "Cost vs. Value Report," using national averages, no common remodeling updates recoup 100 percent of their cost.[1] The report included bathroom remodels (which recouped only 70 percent of their cost), major kitchen remodels (59 percent), and vinyl window replacements (74 percent).

Let's take a closer look at the numbers of how this dynamic plays out. Assume, for example, you are the owner of a home valued at $300,000. You choose to replace all of your home's obsolete windows with new upscale vinyl windows. We can assume the job costs around $16,000 but adds only 74 percent of that cost—about $11,900— to the resale value of the house. In this scenario, this improvement would add $11,900 divided by $300,000 or about 4 percent to the value of the home—but at a cost of $16,000 or more than 5 percent of the home's value. Yes, the renovation increased the home sale value, but spending $16,000 to gain $11,900 is not the best investment of hard-earned money. The scenario is the same if we are talking about new windows, an updated kitchen, or a remodeled bathroom.

When you hear all of the suggestions on how to improve your home's value, be sure to look for data supporting the claim to ensure that any upgrades are truly a worthwhile investment. Only in a few rare cases do upgrades justify the expense, and for the vast majority, a major renovation will not add more value to the sales price of a home than the cost of the upgrade.

HIGHLIGHT VALUE

To sell a house for its full value, or roughly 5 percent to 10 percent above the expected sales price, and maximize the profits for the seller, we need to highlight the home's attributes that add value and which are not found in every home. These attributes are the differentiators and the bonuses that make a house unique to buyers and help us match the home with the best ready, willing, and able buyer. In this section, we will cover a few attributes that have been proven to add value to homes. These attributes are usually not specifically highlighted by either real estate agents or appraisers, but each represents an opportunity to capture the value of these features and can be expected to increase the home's selling price by several percent, which we know can translate to a meaningful total dollar figure. Value can be hidden, and wise sellers know how to identify and highlight these areas of value because value to the buyer translates to profit for the seller.

Green energy ratings

Green energy ratings for homes are one attribute shown to increase a home's value beyond the cost of obtaining it. Green energy ratings show that a home has met a measurable threshold in its level of energy efficiency. A better score means the home uses less energy than comparable homes. A home that is poorly built, with gaps in the exterior walls and thin insulation, would be expected to have higher heating and cooling costs than a similar but better-built home; the conditioned air and embodied energy more easily escapes the poorly built home than the tightly sealed, well-built home.

Today, many green energy rating programs exist. The Home Energy Rating System (HERS), Leadership in Energy and Environmental Design (LEED) for Homes, GreenPoint Rated, and Green Globes all certify homes using similar systems. Other organizations provide more specific certifications, such as the US Environmental Protection Agency's (EPA) Indoor airPLUS and WaterSense programs, which focus on indoor air quality and water efficiency, respectively, and the US Department of Energy's ENERGY STAR certified homes program for new construction homes. The common goal across these programs is to improve energy and water efficiency, improve indoor living conditions, and reduce other environmental impacts.

To understand how these programs work, let's look at one program in more detail. The HERS program evaluates the energy efficiency of homes by comparing the home's energy performance with other comparable homes and then generating a rating—a HERS Index Score. A score of 100 indicates energy efficiency comparable to a newly constructed home in 2006. A score of zero equates to a net zero home or a home that produces as much energy as it consumes.

A typical resale home has a score near 130,[2] which indicates that it is 30 percent less efficient than a newly built home in 2006. The simplicity of a single score allows for ease of comparability across different homes, just as a car buyer can look at the mileage performance on the labels of new cars.

The HERS rating system was developed by the Residential Energy Services Network (RESNET) and introduced in 2006. It has become a standard for federal government agencies in the United States and is recognized by the Department of Energy, the Department of Housing and Urban Development, and the EPA.[3]

Developing a HERS rating requires a comprehensive energy performance assessment of the home by a certified RESNET Home Energy Rater. Using specialized equipment, such as a blower door, an infrared camera, a duct leakage tester, and a combustion analyzer, the rater will identify the amount and location of air leaks in the building envelope, leakage from HVAC ducts, and the effectiveness of insulation inside walls and ceilings. The results of the evaluation will determine the HERS rating. In addition to providing a score, most rating programs also provide the building owner with ideas on how to improve the building's performance.

This score, the additional information about the home, and the third-party verification of energy performance have been proven to add value to homes. Several studies have shown green-rated homes to have higher sale value than comparable homes, although the impact varies by region. A 2018 study in California estimated that green-rated homes sell for over 2 percent more than similar homes.[4] The author looked at sales of green-rated homes as identified in regional multiple listing service (MLS) databases and then found comparable homes and examined the difference in pricing, adjusting for other changes—a paired-sales analysis.

Studies in other regions or using other analytical techniques, such as regression analysis, showed similar results. A previous analysis in California found certified homes selling for 2 percent to 5 percent more. A 2015 paired-sales analysis in Washington, DC, estimated an average green premium of 3.5 percent. And a 2017 study in Austin, Texas, estimated a 6 percent premium.[5]

The premium in the range of 2 percent to 5 percent over comparable homes makes sense. The certifications and high ratings indicate a certain level of construction in the house and also signal that the home has lower energy costs. These lower energy costs translate into lower total operating costs for the house, which, in turn, means a home buyer could actually afford a more expensive house.

Some quick math helps to illustrate the benefit. Let's assume the green home saves the owner an average of $50 per month on energy and water costs. Assuming the home would be financed with a 30-year fixed rate loan at 5 percent interest, the $50 per month saved on energy could be used toward the mortgage payment. The $50 would allow the homeowner to purchase $9,300 more house while keeping their expenses the same relative to a less energy-efficient home. In this light, the price premiums for green homes appear surprisingly logical.

Unfortunately, this area is not well understood by many in the real estate industry and especially by those selling resale homes. New home builders understand the benefits, and several ensure their buyers do as well, using illustrated cutaways in model homes to compare different building methods and how theirs is superior (and why you should buy a home from them, of course!).

It is possible, though, to highlight these benefits. Most multiple listing services have options to add details on green energy features. As one example, the residential data form of the MLS serving the Raleigh–Durham–Chapel Hill, North Carolina, area (the Triangle MLS) has a field for green certification and another for a HERS rating. The MLS also has fields for 25 different green-building features, including LED lighting, locally sourced materials, passive solar design, a sealed attic, a sealed crawl space, solar hot water, programmable thermostats, and even electric car charging stations. These features can also be mentioned in marketing materials for the house and highlighted during showings, similar to how new home builders show off their features.

In the context of differentiators and bonuses, any green building ratings should be highlighted; these ratings could add 2 percent, 3 percent, or even 5 percent to the value of a home. Given that green features are usually built into a new house, the benefit here comes from communicating the rating and what it means to potential buyers. For homes without a formal rating, the cost to have a home energy auditor rate your home will be several hundred dollars, depending on the size and complexity of the work. This is a reasonable investment for the potential of recouping several thousand dollars in a higher sales price.

Solar panels

Solar panels have also been shown to add value to homes beyond the cost of installing them, but the level of value added varies significantly by region. Solar panels, or more specifically, photovoltaic (PV) cells, convert sunlight to electricity. To some, solar panel installations are ugly; to others, they add unnecessary load to the roof of a house, make roof replacements more difficult, and require regular maintenance. But unlike green energy ratings, which are invisible, solar panels are a physical feature of the home. Installation of a solar panel array is a physical improvement similar to a finished basement or the addition of a sunroom. Physical work was completed and a physical object was added to the home.

Solar panels, though, differ from the others in that they can lower the home's operating costs by producing electricity. The cost-benefit comparison here varies tremendously by state, region, and utility area. On its own, without subsidies, the costs of a roof-mounted solar system do not provide an attractive return on investment in most situations. The US government has provided tax benefits for solar power (and other energy systems), although these can vary as policies adjust and change. Each state has its own set of energy and environmental priorities and approach, which, in turn, impact what regulatory or financial support is provided to homeowners who install rooftop PV arrays. Some states provide subsidies to homeowners through tax credits or other mechanisms. Others support alternative approaches to energy generation and provide little or no support to homeowners. Local governments and utilities also have programs that shape the net cost to a homeowner to install a PV system.

Once installed, though, these systems provide electricity to the homeowner and sometimes to the local power grid and can lower the home's monthly electricity costs. Again, the level of benefits and specific value to any individual homeowner varies so much that a standard answer other than "it depends" holds no value. However, because the buyer will be purchasing a house with the solar system already installed, that system can represent a hefty benefit for them worth paying for.

Considered as a whole, though, solar panels do add value to the home and the data are backing this up. According to one analysis looking at the premiums of homes with rooftop solar installations, having a PV system can add 3 percent to 6 percent to the sales price, with a value increase in the range of $10,000–$20,000.[6] As a physical upgrade, solar panels provide ongoing benefits and, in some regions, additional cachet to buyers who desire a home with solar panels.

One caveat is whether the solar panels are owned or leased by the seller. Owned solar panels are generally a positive in many regions across the United States. Leased solar panels, however, can be more problematic. Although the installation of leased solar panels could have made excellent financial sense for the owners who made the decision, selling homes with leased arrays can complicate the sale, because the seller and buyer have to manage either transferring the lease arrangement or terminating the lease.

Thinking in terms of differentiator and bonuses, solar panels provide a way to distinguish properties from similar properties with no solar panels. For some buyers, this could be a strong selling point.

TREES

Another underappreciated source of value are mature trees near the home or along the street. Mature trees, defined roughly as trees larger than what could be purchased from a landscaper, can add value to homes.

New construction homes tend to have no large trees near the home. A common scene across the United States are rows and rows of houses with barely more than a few small bushes in front of each home in newly constructed neighborhoods. This barren landscape contrasts with neighborhoods built in the 1990s or earlier, where trees have grown in and around the houses. Trees provide a pleasant and relaxed feeling to the neighborhood and one people find more comfortable.

The University of Washington has compiled a list of studies showing the value of mature trees on home values. Although the development costs are greater for lots where trees are conserved, builders can recover these costs through higher sales prices and faster sales of houses on those wooded lots. These researchers also estimated that the presence of larger trees in yards and those placed along the street could add from 3 percent to 15 percent to home values throughout neighborhoods.[7] In another example, a study published in 2013 showed that in six Cincinnati, Ohio, neighborhoods, the average value of the tree canopy accounted for nearly 11 percent of the price of the homes in those neighborhoods.[8]

The value of mature trees is not limited to a single lot or to just the United States. In the United Kingdom, studies have shown how mature trees add between 5 percent and 18 percent to a home's value.[9]

These findings make sense. Compare the visual of the barren new home subdivision landscape to the dense canopies of Myers Park, in Charlotte, North Carolina; Park Slope, in Brooklyn, New York; and parts of northwest Washington, DC. These neighborhoods feature both stunning trees and high home values.[10]

Mature trees have a positive influence on the price of the home relative to similar homes without trees. This value persists despite the additional time and maintenance associated with large trees on a property. As a differentiator, an old live oak in the front yard or the bountiful pecan tree in the back can make a major difference in the selling price of a home.

TRUE VALUE

Traditional home improvement projects rarely pay back more than the cost of the project. This lack of a financial return is a symptom of the continual investment in a depreciating asset required to simply maintain its value.

Value, though, can be found in other attributes, especially those that money cannot buy or that can save money for the buyer. We have seen how energy-efficient homes, solar panels, and mature trees can add value to a home in contrast to most other home improvements. So, what should you do as a seller? My recommendation is simply to do your homework. Do not undertake a home improvement project without understanding both the costs and potential selling price increase the improvement could provide. Of course, expensive upgrades will increase the selling price of the home, but the price increase will likely not be enough to recoup the investment in the project. Understanding the difference between price and value is key to knowing how to sell your home for its full value and maximizing the profits you earn.

PART 2

PREPARING FOR THE SALE

In a competitive market, successful products win by providing excellent value to customers. This is no different in the residential real estate market. One major difference is that a new product purchased from a store is brand new, wrapped in original packaging and without any scratches, scuffs, or marks. A resale home is a used product and shows wear and tear. As the seller, it is your job to help buyers look past any wear to see the benefits of the product itself. We need to make your home into a product that excites potential buyers.

Most home buyers are willing to pay top dollar for high-quality homes that appear like new. This doesn't necessarily mean that a home needs to have all of the high-end upgrades and finishes but, rather, that it shows well and that the buyers could see themselves living in it. It is the buyer's perspective that informs where you should spend your time and energy preparing your house for sale. And a full-price buyer's perspective is pretty simple: They want a clean home in good condition with as few surprises as possible where they can live their life in the way they want to.

We'll discuss where your efforts should be focused to maximize the selling price with minimal investment. Starting from the curb and moving inside the house, we'll cover how to hook potential buyers with a strong first impression and then how to keep them wowed once they're inside the home. These chapters cover practical, affordable actions that have been proven to improve the sales price of your home.

FIRST IMPRESSIONS: CURB APPEAL

The buyer's first impression starts with the curb appeal of a home—its appearance from the street. Their initial reaction here will influence every subsequent step in their evaluation of the home. Improving curb appeal is one of the oldest and most often repeated recommendations by real estate agents, and for good reason. According to the academic research, a home with high curb appeal can sell for 10 percent or even 20 percent more than comparable homes lacking the same appeal. This makes sense. A positive first impression sets the buyer's mood as they tour the rest of the house. The impact of this first impression and the walk from the curb to the front door are so powerful that real estate investors sometimes call it the Golden Path. This path can sell a house before the buyer even enters the front door. The magnitude of the impact makes getting it right crucial to selling your house at full value.

Curb appeal is everything related to the property's visible exterior. This includes the front lawn, the driveway, landscaping, and the home's exterior. Here, the small details such as potted plants, a welcome mat, and a polished mailbox make a difference. For some sellers, the amount of work to properly prepare the Golden Path can seem daunting, but we will break it down into a few digestible pieces. The first step is to understand the concept of curb appeal in its two primary components: the home's exterior and the landscaping.

EXTERIOR

The exterior is the part of your home's structure that a potential buyer can see from the street. This includes the type and condition of wall materials such as brick or siding; the color and condition of wall and trim paint; its coordination with other features such as the bricks and roof shingles; the type of windows and shutters; the type of front door and storm door; the type of porch supports; and the type and condition of a front garage door.[1] Special features, such as a deep front porch or a special roof, can increase the appeal of the home, while large visible satellite dishes and garages converted into living rooms detract.

If you visualize each of these elements, you should be able to intuitively understand how they contribute to the level of curb appeal for the home. Although peeling paint or dented aluminum siding is an obvious negative, we would argue so is the 2004-ish rose-colored siding with cranberry shutters—especially in a neighborhood where the surrounding houses are a more typical East Coast beige or gray. Look closely at the front of your house from the sidewalk or across the street. What stands out? Is one element an obvious problem? If so, that's where you start cleaning, repairing, or replacing. Compare it with your neighbors' houses. Does your house look modern and appealing or dated? Consult with your real estate agent. They see hundreds of homes each year and should be able to guide you to the most crucial improvements.

LANDSCAPING

The degree and condition of landscaping is what sets one home apart from another. Factors in landscaping include tree cover and quality, grass quality, the volume and diversity of plants around the home, the maintenance of the plants, the concrete's condition, the size and amount of softscapes and hardscapes, and finally, the design coordination among all of these elements.[2]

Pause here and think about these landscape factors of your home and your neighborhood. Is your home the one with the best lawn, watered every night and mowed weekly? You can surely think of well-maintained yards on the block where the grass is immaculate, the trees are well kept, and the sidewalk and driveway are in like-new condition. These homes brighten up any neighborhood.

Or is your home the one with the foot-tall weeds and the flower-bed full of dry stems? Does your home have bushes that appear to not have been trimmed in decades? Are parts of the driveway covered with years of accumulated pine needles, weeds pushing up between the seams, and oil stains from an old car?

Well-kept landscaping varies in many degrees as well, with more advanced landscaping having more value to buyers. A basic level of landscaping, common with new homes and often a last-minute consideration of contractors, includes essentially a bare yard and a bed of mulch in front of the house, with a few simple shrubs, perhaps all of the same species, planted there. A higher level of landscaping would keep the same plantings around the foundation of the house but add in a tree or two and an additional island with plantings of flowers or other greenery in an attractive location. A third level of design sophistication would include coordinated, multiple plantings around the home's foundation for an attractive edge to the home and multiple trees and curved island beds.

Your buyers will see the same thing you do when they approach the house for the first time. You have only one opportunity to make that first impression, so make sure your house stands out in a good way.

WHAT THE RESEARCH SHOWS

Data support our assertion of the value of curb appeal. One study, completed by researchers at Texas Tech University in 2012, looked precisely at this topic.[3] The researchers examined 75 houses in the Lubbock, Texas, area that sold around the same time. These houses were mostly the typical brick ranch-style homes common to the area, and most of the houses were built in the 1960s. To estimate the impact of curb appeal, the researchers developed separate evaluation forms for the house and for the landscaping. They then asked designers and other home professionals to use the forms to evaluate the curb appeal for each home and its landscaping and to assign each home a rating of "Low," "Average," or "High." These ratings were then analyzed with other more traditional house pricing factors, such as sales price, house size, lot size, price per square foot, and so on, to estimate the impact of curb appeal on a home's sales price.

For the homes in the studied population, the researchers estimated the difference in home value between a home with a low curb appeal rating and one with an average rating to be 8.6 percent, or more than $12,000. The sales price difference between homes sold with an average rating and those sold with a high rating was 7.4 percent. And the difference between a "low" rated home and a "high" rated home was more than 16 percent—a value of $23,000!

Breaking down the total scores into the two components of landscaping and house appeal, the researchers found similar relationships as scores moved from low to average to high. The value of the landscaping and the value of the house appeal were roughly equal. Both matter to maximize the sales price of a home.

This study is not the only one to develop an estimate of the impact of enhanced curb appeal. Earlier studies by researchers at Virginia Tech[4] and at Clemson[5] produced similar results showing that improving a home's curb appeal could increase the selling price by more than 7 percent. This is a significant increase in the value a home seller could realize with comparatively little effort. Our premise that a home's price could be improved by 5 percent to 10 percent over an initial expected selling price continues to be validated.

WHAT TO DO ABOUT IT

To start, look at your property from the curb, as if you were a buyer pulling up to look at the house. Write down everything you see that could be improved. You don't have to fix everything, but you should do what you can to make your house appear inviting. Start from the curb and work your way toward the front door. Look at the sidewalk—is it dark or does it look new? Is there a mailbox by the street—is it polished and any plants around it neat? Is the yard edged and mowed? Is the landscaping maintained? Is the front of the house visible and clean? Is the roof clean? Are there any flowers or plants near the front entry to greet potential buyers? And, finally, is the front door and especially the knob or handle in excellent condition?

Your landscaping can be drastically improved with just a few small touches, and they don't even have to be permanent. When selling our Raleigh townhome, we focused on improving the curb appeal where we could. Prior to showing the home and having it photographed, we purchased two simple boxwood plants and simple clay pots to place on our small front porch. This small detail made a big impact in enhancing the entrance of the home. Your yard might need a bed of mulch or a potted tree, or you might need to hire someone to remove all the weeds. You don't have to redesign the entire front yard; just make it look clean and appealing.

Update any obviously dated structures on the front of the house. Porch supports are an example of a subtle element that is obvious from the curb and can make an initial positive or negative impression. Intricate metal supports, often painted white or black, were common in the 1960s and look every bit of that age today, when more contemporary supports, such as those in the Craftsman style or boxed rather than curved, are preferred. Low-cost and readily available column wraps can quickly change the look of these porch supports, and they are not as expensive or as difficult to replace as you'd think. The selection of items like these and others can quickly improve a home's exterior and improve the home's curb appeal—and its potential selling price.

Repair any obvious damage to the home with special focus on the front door. Items to repair could include wood rot on the trim or a crack in the driveway concrete. If your paint is flaking, repaint. If your siding is old and cracked, paint over it or replace it. If the front door is broken or dented, replace it.

Finally, clean the exterior of the house thoroughly—and keep it clean. Power washing can be an efficient way to quickly improve a home's curb appeal. Washing off years of accumulated grime and dullness from a roof and walls can make an astonishing change to a house. This includes the concrete driveway and any sidewalks in front of the house. Like a home's exterior, sidewalks and driveways fade and become dirty, and cleaning these areas makes the important first impression even more positive. An exterior cleaning should include washing all windows inside and out. As light reflects off the exterior, clean windows create a certain shine that some buyers find attractive. Clean windows also let more light into the house, which further increases the home's appeal.

Before any scheduled tours or open houses, sweep the porch and the driveway. The front porch should be spotless prior to any home buyer visits. This effort will pay off because of the power of a positive first impression.

Given the potential positive impact it can provide, particularly on the sales price, curb appeal is one of my top must-do recommendations for selling a home for more. You can never re-create the first impression of any buyer, so make sure that first time counts.

I COULD LIVE HERE

One common recommendation offered by real estate agents to homeowners is to consider staging their home. *Staging* typically means renting idealized furniture and décor to make the home more appealing for a buyer. However, the process more generally involves creating a blank canvas that the buyer can imagine themselves and their family living in. That requires you to make the property less personal and to make sure the buyer feels like they are walking through their own future home rather than someone else's. This process starts by removing your personal items. It might require you to paint an accent wall or several entire rooms in a more neutral or inviting color. Depending on your goals, it could also include renting those overstuffed armchairs, baskets of wicker balls, and fat candles. Ultimately, to sell for full value, you must ensure that your home is less obviously lived in so your buyer can easily picture themselves making it their home.

DEPERSONALIZING

Removing uniquely personal items is the first step to convert a home into a house. Although depersonalizing can be difficult for you as the home seller, the lack of personal items is crucial to helping buyers visualize themselves living there.

Imagine you are a buyer and you walk into three identical homes. The first is vacant, ready for new occupants. The second is lightly staged, with only a few pieces of furniture in rooms throughout the house and a few additional items in the bathrooms and kitchen to provide an aspirational environment. And then you walk into the third house, the one that is lived in.

In this third home, you are greeted by a metal pig at the front door. As you walk in, you quickly see the pork theme that peppers the house—statues of hogs and pigs, prints of bacon and ham, and various other themed décor. The downstairs is obviously home to a large dog with its bed and dishes occupying a corner. Hanging on the wall behind the dining table is an oil painting of an old home, perhaps the family homestead. At the top of the stairwell is a portrait of what appears to be an old family patriarch. One bedroom upstairs is clearly for the family's toddler—with toys scattered around the floor and crayon markings on the wall of the adjoining bathroom. The master bedroom closet is filled with women's clothes, shoes, and accessories. The bonus room has a sofa that looks as though it barely survived many years of college. And on the deck outside are two grills, one charcoal and the second a Big Green Egg.

Walking into the third house feels like walking into someone's home when they are not there, like you're sneaking through their lives. It feels somewhat creepy, since you were not really invited. You spend more time trying to figure out the lives of the current residents than imagining yourself moving in. What's with all the pigs? Are they moving because they are having a second child? How does a Big Green Egg compare to a gas grill?

Buyers will have a more difficult time visualizing themselves living in that home relative to the vacant home or the staged home. The unprepared home is highly personalized and requires more work from the buyer to understand what the house actually offers. The clutter throughout an occupied home also detracts from the buyer's visualization.

As a seller, you should be deliberate in depersonalizing your home before it is listed for sale. This means removing the obvious personal items—the family photos, the college diplomas, the wall stickers in the children's room—but much of the additional home décor as well, including paintings and other wall hangings and even most of the books on the shelves. Each of these items provides a sense of individuality and makes the house your home, which is precisely the feeling you want to avoid when selling a home. You are selling the house as a product, and the buyer must be able to easily imagine making your house their home.

THE RIGHT COLOR

Another classic real estate agent recommendation is "paint your interior a neutral color," such as off-white or beige, to not offend any potential buyers. Although this is considered safe and conservative advice, it has the potential to leave money on the table. A pleasant pop of color can add value to your home.

In today's world, buyers are starting their searches more and more often online. Color provides a chance for home sellers to stand out from their competition. Choosing the right colors allows key rooms to look more up-to-date and appealing than neutral-colored spaces. Fortunately, using the power of big data and computer visual recognition, the impact of colors on home sales prices can be quantified.

In 2017 Zillow conducted a study evaluating 32,000 photos of sold homes and compared the sales prices of similar homes painted different colors.[1] At the time of the study, shades of blue, including light shades of powder blue and periwinkle, were associated with an increase in a home's sales price of more than $5,000. White or off-white bathrooms sold for more than $4,000 less than average. Blues in the dining room and kitchen also increased a home's sales price by nearly $2,000.

Just as hitting a color trend can help the sales value of a home, missing the trend can hurt it. Zillow's study found the use of outdated colors, such as a mustard-colored wall in the kitchen, would decrease a home's value by more than $800.

The use of color is a risk but one that can provide a reward to savvy homeowners at a minimal cost. For those who are not savvy or just looking for a simple recommendation, the old classic of a bland neutral color won't hurt the sale, but the seller could miss out on a potential bonus to the sales price.

DECLUTTERING

Decluttering the home takes depersonalizing one step deeper. In addition to removing personal items, removing other, more general "stuff" opens the home up even more and further helps the buyers visualize living there. The benefits of thoroughly cleaning and decluttering your house are less obvious than other slam-dunk recommendations, such as improving curb appeal. We know the data clearly support higher sales values for homes with better curb appeal, but the relationship between a clean and decluttered home and a higher sales price is less clear. However, while little direct research has been done in this space, there is abundant indirect evidence for other benefits of showing a clean and decluttered home when selling.

First, a clean and decluttered house enables potential buyers to better visualize living in the home than a messy and cluttered house would. Next, strong evidence exists showing how clean and decluttered homes provide the occupants a wide variety of health benefits. For potential buyers, this sense of a potential healthy home environment can be seen during their visits to cleaner homes. Finally, a clean and decluttered home simply photographs better, so the home has a reasonable chance of being shortlisted by potential buyers.

One fascinating study comes courtesy of UCLA's Center on Everyday Lives of Families (CELF), which researches and documents the everyday home life of working middle-class families. In 2009 CELF sent a team of professional archaeologists, anthropologists, and other social scientists to study the home lives of 30 dual-income middle-class families in Los Angeles, California. The lives of these participants were meticulously recorded and documented.[2]

Two findings are relevant to preparing a house for sale. In the first, researchers estimated that nearly 75 percent of the families packed their garages so full with belongings that there was no room for cars.[3] Their garages were filled with rejected furniture, boxes, and other items. Other larger surveys put the total number of Americans who cannot use their garage in the 20 percent range. Yet another survey found nearly half of Americans encountered problems with being able to park in their garage.[4] When decluttering, be sure to also declutter the garage. Buyers do look at the garage when considering homes, and it should not look like a storage unit. All clutter should be moved out of the home. Here, it makes sense to use a storage unit to temporarily house items worth keeping while the house is being shown for sale.

A second finding from the CELF study has more serious implications. The researchers examined participants' levels of diurnal cortisol, a stress hormone, through saliva samples and found a link between clutter and increased cortisol levels of women in the study. Using the same set of families, the researchers asked to tour their homes and recorded words relating to the home environment. The researchers looked for words related to clutter, such as *messy, junk, unorganized, disaster, trash,* and *chaotic.* They also looked for key words in three other categories: unfinished house (*repair, fix, project, redecorate*), restful environment (*relax, lounge, soothing, peaceful*), and nature (*outside, patio, deck, plant, trees*). The researchers then correlated the words with both the husband's and the wife's moods. The husbands were not impacted by messy homes.[5] For the wives in the study, however, a cluttered home led to higher levels of stress hormones and increased depressive moods.

Our brains and our bodies require order to operate, and this desire for order and coordination extend into our home environments. When our bodies are no longer able to manage the complexity of our living environments, we become stressed. Clutter and its associated stress are known to lead to the release of cortisol in our bodies. And cortisol can increase tension, anxiety, and unhealthy habits.[6] Elevated cortisol levels are known to increase blood pressure, heart rate, blood sugars, and fats in the blood.

And this can happen to potential home buyers when they walk through a cluttered home.

Clutter causes stress to the body and distracts the mind. For home sellers looking to maximize the sale of their home, causing buyers additional stress is clearly not the way to do it. By cleaning the clutter, you can help potential buyers see the home with a clear mind in a calming environment.

Clutter also represents a practical challenge for home sales professionals. One appraiser, asked to complete the routine task of measuring the square footage of a home, shared his experience of not being able to accurately measure rooms because junk lined every wall from floor to ceiling. The appraiser literally could not see any walls to accurately measure the size of the room!

In another example, one real estate agent was asked to help an elderly owner sell their home. After the agent asked to walk around the house to see how it looked, he was forced to step sideways down the hall, because the owner kept every newspaper he had received for decades. The home was crowded with old newspapers throughout. Needless to say, most buyers visiting a home lined with piles of newspapers could miss some of the more positive aspects of the house.

I doubt your home has a "hoarder" level of clutter, but removing any clutter you do have will make the open house and showing process much more pleasant—and effective—for your potential buyers.

CLEANING

Cleaning a home can add value in the same way decluttering can. While no data exist to explicitly link a cleaner home with a higher sales price, a dirty home conveys unwellness and can be off-putting to potential buyers. A home's cleanliness also highlights key features while minimizing any distractions that dirt, dust, or smells could cause.

Most people recognize the health implications of a dirty home either consciously or unconsciously. As we've seen in the previous section, a dirty and cluttered home causes mental distraction, physical stress, and an overall feeling of unwellness. It is crucial that a home for sale be completely decluttered and deep cleaned inside and out—especially the most impactful areas, such as the bathrooms, kitchen, and bedrooms. Cleaning and decluttering also allows the buyer to see the home in the best light possible so they can visualize what it could be like for them to live there.

STAGING

Despite an entire industry touting the anecdotal benefits of a staged home, it is difficult finding data to support the idea that staged homes sell for higher prices than homes that are not staged.

However, data does support the assertion that staged homes sell *faster* than unstaged homes.

Complicating the decision to stage a home are the associated costs. First, there are the direct costs of a stager's services and the rental of the furnishings used. Second, a staged home is generally assumed to not be in use by the seller and, therefore, represents a carrying cost each month of either a mortgage payment due, a rent payment not realized, or interest not realized by funds being tied up in the investment. These costs must be compared with the benefit of either a quicker sale or higher sales price.

Another factor to consider is the trade-off between an empty home, with no furniture in it, and a staged home. Some experts believe the empty home appears larger to buyers who would be willing to pay more for this perceived extra space. Again, this benefit must be evaluated against any perceived benefits of staging.

Academics have attempted to understand the relationship between staging and home prices and have found no strong relationship. In a 2015 study, researchers at three schools in Virginia developed an experiment to test buyer preferences.[7] To do this, the researchers developed a model of a virtual home and then created variations of the interior. The researchers created three staging versions: one that would be considered well staged with stylish furniture, a second version not staged and with ugly furniture, and a third version with no furniture. The researchers then asked their participants for an estimate of the home's value.

As a whole, the participants did not provide data to indicate they would be willing to pay more for the staged homes than for the unstaged homes. The participants liked the homes that were staged better, but they were not willing to pay more for them. Interestingly, the researchers later asked the participants what they thought others would pay for the homes. The participants responded that they believed others would pay a higher price for the staged homes, but they themselves would not.

This gap between the reality ("I wouldn't pay more") and the perception ("I believe others would pay more") of potential home buyers is part of the misunderstanding that perpetuates the continued advice by real estate agents and others that staging helps to sell homes at a higher price.

The Real Estate Staging Association claims the benefits of staging to be a shorter time on the market and lower carrying costs rather than an increased sales price. According to its analysis of more than a thousand homes, unstaged homes spent nearly 184 days on the market, whereas homes staged prior to listing were sold after only 23 days—a difference of nearly 90 percent less time on the market.[8]

What does all of this mean? Staging does not necessarily increase the selling price of a home, although the property might sell more quickly. However, the costs of staging could outweigh the associated benefits of a quick sale. That balance is something you'll have to determine for your own personal situation.

MY RECOMMENDATIONS

First, repaint the interior mostly in neutral colors, but pick a pleasant and appealing accent color to set your house apart from its online competition. Next, ensure the home is clean and decluttered or, even better, mostly empty. Finally, consider minimal staging at a very low cost. Minimal staging would mean something such as a table and chairs in the dining room, a bedroom set in the master bedroom, and perhaps some signaling accessories, such as a basket with towels in the master bath. You might include a cookbook on a stand or a container with wooden utensils in the kitchen and maybe a few other items to convey the use of the space. More staging will not hurt the sale and should be considered as a trade-off of cost and time.

PART 3

MARKETING YOUR HOME

No matter how similar a house may look to its neighbors, inside and out, each house is unique. Even if a unit is constructed identically to the unit next door, its location a few feet closer or farther from the subdivision entrance, the park, the clubhouse, or the highway will set it apart. The views, the neighbors, and the time it takes to walk from the lot entrance to the front door are all different.

For any unique product, the buyer is also unique: Only one person can buy your home at any one time. That buyer must be ready to buy—be in the market for a house. The buyer must also be willing to buy—be interested in your particular house enough to make it their home. And they must be able to buy—have financing available with either a mortgage approval or cash in hand.

Finding a buyer for a seller is, at its core, a classic matching problem. How do we quickly match a unique product—your house for sale—with one ready, willing, and able buyer? The residential real estate market consists of millions of buyers and sellers, and buyers are available all the time for any property. And any property will sell at a very low price. To sell for more, though, we need to be deliberate and find the right buyer—that one ready, willing, and able buyer offering the best combination of price and terms for the product.

In this section, we will explore the specifics of marketing your home. We will start with an overview of the process the home buyer usually goes through and then build an approach that aligns with how the buyer purchases a home.

THE BUYER'S
PERSPECTIVE

To sell a house for maximum profit, we must understand our customer: the buyer. Buyers tend to do the same actions when purchasing a home. Knowing how they buy will help us focus on actions to help them want to buy the house you are selling.

When you consider a home sale from the buyer's perspective, several points immediately become obvious. First, price is one of the initial filtering criteria. Buyers looking for homes in the $200,000 range typically will not look for homes in the $600,000 range and vice versa; buyers look for homes that are within their preferred range. Next, buyers look at the structure and location.

There is not much the seller can do about the price. As we've already discussed, your home's price will fit into a logical and comparable range. We believe you can sell a home for 5 percent to 10 percent above the home's expected sales price, but you are unlikely to attract buyers if your home is priced significantly above its true value.

There are actions you can take to make the home attractive to buyers, as we discussed in the previous part. Although you could change the structure of your home through extensive remodeling or constructing an addition, these are expensive and time-consuming modifications, and they almost always have a financial return less than the investment. And there's nothing you can do about location.

What this means for you as the seller is that there is not much you can do to influence which buyers are looking for a property like yours. However, you can take actions to ensure that those buyers who are looking for a property like yours can find it. You can also affect how well your home stands out in the early stages of the buyer's search— by highlighting the unique features of your property in the listing and marketing materials. Finally, you can also affect how comfortable the buyer feels buying from you.

This brings us back to our matching problem: How do we connect a ready, willing, and able buyer with our product? Although this process is not exactly like trying to find a needle in a haystack, it has the potential to feel this way if the house is not marketed effectively. To understand how to market the home, we need to understand with some specificity the process buyers go through before purchasing a home. Fortunately for us, though, most buyers go through a similar experience when preparing to buy a home.

THE BUYER FUNNEL

As a whole, buyers today come to the market as the most informed buyers in history. Detailed property information is readily available online to potential buyers sitting at home. Previous generations depended on a local real estate agent to share details of homes for sale. Tax records, deeds, plats, and permits were located at various government offices. Today, all of this information is available with just a few clicks.

These buyers will use this information to narrow down their potential home purchase to just a handful of houses—often well before they visit the property. The process of considering hundreds of homes, circling through them while narrowing the options, then closing on a single one is referred to as the *buyer funnel*. By understanding this process, we can market the home at each step along the way and, by doing so, match the best buyer with the marketed property. The buyer funnel starts with conducting research and then developing a shortlist of homes and comparing them. Buyers then visit only the top choices, putting in an offer on a single house before finally closing on it.

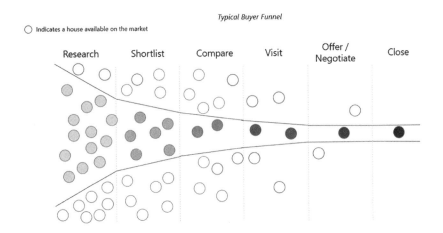

Figure 6.1. The buyer funnel

Research

At the research stage, the buyer will establish a price range they can afford, identify the features they must have, and get a feel for what kinds of properties are available. They develop the starting point for either where they want to live or what sort of house they want. They look for a safe neighborhood. They look for homes that are close to their jobs. They look for homes in good school districts or even in proximity to a specific school.

At the same time, buyers start to understand what is available for them and what they will and will not accept. The number of bedrooms is important to many buyers. Older home buyers may want a one-story home or ground-level condominium. Younger buyers may only want a house close to public transportation, restaurants, and bars. Some buyers may have RVs, boats, or exotic pets that are not allowed by communities with homeowners associations. Once buyers understand their preferences, they begin to create a shortlist of homes.

The shortlist

The shortlisted homes will meet most of the buyer's preferences, and buyers will become more focused in their search at this point. For instance, they may get as specific as looking for a home "under $400,000 in school district X, with at least four bedrooms and three bathrooms, no more than a 30-minute commute from the office downtown, at least 2,000 square feet, and not built in the 1960s or '70s." It is no coincidence that many real estate websites offer the capability to search for homes with exactly these criteria.

Comparison

Next is the comparison phase, where buyers evaluate specific homes in more detail. They start to look beyond the basic attributes that can be filtered on a search page. They'll start asking questions such as these: Has the house been updated? Is there a fence for our dog? What is the setup for the kitchen and living area? Is the laundry room upstairs or downstairs? Could our piano fit in this house? How close is this house to the community pool? Is the yard well kept? What are the neighboring houses like? Once these questions are answered as well as possible with the information available online, the home buyer then begins to consider which homes to visit.

Visiting properties

The fourth step in the process is planning a visit. At this stage, the buyer targets specific homes that they would consider for purchase. For most buyers, visits are time intensive and usually require the friction of coordinating with an agent and, through them, the sellers. Depending on how well they know the area and their purchase preferences, they may visit just a few houses. An average home buyer sees about 10 homes prior to making an offer.[1]

The offer

After visiting homes and finding the one they love, the buyers will submit an offer and begin negotiation.

Closing the deal

If the offer is accepted, the buyer will usually conduct some level of due diligence on the property.[2] If no deal-breaking issues arise and the transaction proceeds, there is usually still some negotiation as to what is specifically included in the transaction and requests for some repairs to be completed. Household items, such as curtains, curtain rods, refrigerators, and chandeliers, can become points of negotiation or contention in the transaction. Once the due diligence, negotiations, financing, and any other requested actions are complete, the transaction can then close.

Most buyers make offers on only one home at a time, so the home you are selling must stand out from the competition at every stage along the buyer funnel. To do that, you must carefully consider how the property is marketed, with two specific goals of highlighting the unique features of your house and reducing the buyer's perceived risk.

HIGHLIGHT DIFFERENTIATORS

As a seller, you should highlight differentiating features of your home throughout every phase of the buyer's funnel, with a special focus on the comparison phase. At this point, your home has met the buyer's initial needs for price, location, and basic structural preferences, but it now faces competition and needs to stand out from other homes on the market. Is the home move-in ready? Does it have air-conditioning? Does it have a private outdoor space?[3] Is it energy efficient? In the comparison phase, buyers look for bonuses, positive features that are not necessarily one of their preferences but that could swing a decision between two similar properties. Examples of bonus features are preferred finishes, such as marble or granite; a preferred number of bathrooms; proximity to shopping; good views; ample storage; and shared community amenities.

It is in this area of differentiators and bonuses where a house can be set apart from others and matched to the right buyer. When the buyer is looking at these details, they are comparing their shortlisted homes to decide which homes to visit. As a seller, this is when we want the house to shine.

Take the example of two homes in a typical neighborhood—in this case, two homes built in the 1990s in a wooded subdivision. One house's listing description starts with something like "Great location at the end of cul-de-sac and close to hospital. This property lives large, with three bedrooms and 3.5 baths." Although this sounds great and is typical of many listings, this same information is available in the property details and adds minimal value to the buyer. And I'm not exactly sure what "living large" means. This description does not differentiate in any way; in reality, this property had been on the market for months longer than an average home in the price range, and the price was being cut to make the sale.

Now, compare that description with this one for a nearby house whose listing started with "Live in a 'tree house'! Great location close to hospital. Porch and deck plus separate deck structure overlooking private backyard with stream." From the perspective of highlighting differentiators and bonuses, these remarks are on point. A porch, multiple decks, a private backyard, and a stream—this combination will appeal to a specific buyer, crucial for the matching process. To maximize the value of a house being sold, you must highlight the differentiators and bonuses to potential buyers.

We'll talk more specifically about the listing in the next chapter, but you should highlight your home's differentiators in all marketing materials, and—as we saw in the previous part—in the home itself.

REDUCING BUYER RISK

Due to uncertainty and a lack of knowledge about the home and the neighborhood, home buyers worry about making a bad decision or an expensive mistake, both of which could lead them to lower their offer or even move on to another property. A home buyer beginning their due diligence knows there is a significant imbalance in knowledge between the seller and the buyer. By reducing that knowledge gap, you can give the home buyer comfort and confidence.

Sellers have more information than the buyer simply because they live in the house. The seller knows that the dogs next door bark all night, that the traffic in front of the house peaks between 7:45 a.m. and 8:10 a.m. because parents are dropping their kids off at the nearby middle school, and that the neighbors two houses down regularly host dinner parties where the guests' cars block off the whole street. Inside the house, the seller knows which power outlet sparks when the iron is plugged into it and where the water leaked from the toilet upstairs onto the living room ceiling below. As the seller, you have this information, and this information is valuable to the buyer.

Imagine a scenario where there are two equal houses on the market but one seller has provided more complete information about the home and the other shares no information. Here, the buyer would be willing to pay more for the house with complete information. Purchasing this home has less downside risk than the home with the unknowns, and therefore, the buyer is more comfortable with the purchase. Would you prefer to purchase a home that you have completed extensive due diligence on, including a survey, home inspection, A/C inspection, title review, and so on, or would you prefer to buy an identical house—at the same total price and terms—at a county auction, with minimal paperwork, no inspection, and no opportunity to cancel the purchase? Given the risk of a costly surprise for scenario B, most rational buyers would choose to purchase the house in scenario A.

The townhome my wife and I bought in Raleigh, North Carolina, was located in a well-known floodplain. As buyers, we knew about the location and its flood zone designation. We did not believe this designation would be a deal-breaker. The owners and their neighbors had lived in the area for years, but we had our concerns, and we had to do additional investigation about the risks of living in this particular floodplain. We learned we were in the 100-year floodplain, which meant that the building had at least a 1 percent chance of a flood equal to or exceeding the base flood elevation in any given year. Our mortgage company was aware of this sort of situation and told us that this level of risk translated to a 26 percent chance of flooding over the life of a 30-year mortgage. We hired a surveyor to confirm the elevation above the flood level. Fortunately, the builder of the townhome had the foresight to position the building well above the expected flood levels. This elevation reduced the likelihood of flood damage to the building even if the area around the townhome flooded. Furthermore, both our home inspector and another builder confirmed there were no visual signs of past flooding, which assured us there was no history of the home flooding—yet. We felt we had a good understanding of the flood risk at the location, and this understanding factored into our calculations for making an offer, because we decided it was a risk we were willing to take at the price we would offer for the townhome.

We did this detailed research on understanding the flood risk because the sellers answered property disclosure form questions about flooding with responses of "no representation" or "unknown," which many buyers will interpret as "I know, but I am not going to tell you." Vague responses like this raise questions about how well the seller actually knows the property and signals to the buyer that this is a seller who could be difficult to work with through the home sale process. For many buyers, just learning that the home was in a flood zone would lead them to find another property. In our case, it resulted in us doing the research on our own and submitting a lower offer. If the sellers had provided this information up front, as we did when we later sold the townhome, the question of flooding risk could have been resolved quickly with good information and resulted in a higher initial offer and probably a higher selling price.

Potentially lowering the value of a home by sharing too much information is a real concern. As we saw in the flood zone disclosure, a negative response to any of the initial property disclosure questions could reduce the value of the property. So, what is the incentive to disclose more information than the absolute minimum required? The incentive is that this information is valuable to prospective purchasers and, done well, sharing it can actually increase the sales price of the home.[4]

In 2006 a University of Connecticut researcher set out to examine how property disclosure forms affect property values. At the time, disclosure forms were not as prevalent across the country, and the impact could be estimated by comparing home values among metropolitan areas. The researchers found that an average seller providing a state-mandated property-condition disclosure statement to a buyer could expect to realize a higher sales price, in the range of 3 percent to 4 percent over the expected value.[5]

So, how can you help your potential buyers reduce the risk associated with the knowledge imbalance?

First, ensure that any mandated property disclosures are complete.

Second, consider providing additional information to help the buyer get to know the property. This additional information could include a copy of the deed, a recent home inspection, a survey, warranties and receipts for appliances that will convey with the house, utility bills, and minutes of recent homeowners association meetings. While not required, volunteering this information for serious buyers can help provide additional comfort as they consider submitting an offer. This sharing also signals that you know the property well and will be a cooperative seller during the closing.

Finally, consider a home warranty. A home warranty provides buyers some degree of coverage should a key system fail either during the sale process or in the years following the sale. Several companies provide home warranties, and each has its own set of specific details. One common home warranty program covers heating systems, air-conditioning and heat pumps, appliances, plumbing, and electrical systems. It also provides the option to purchase coverage for washers and dryers, leaky roofs and pipes, septic systems, and pool equipment. For homes where previous owners may not have maintained their systems, a home warranty could make sense.

Especially if it is a buyer's market at the time of sale, a home warranty paid for by the seller could provide the additional risk coverage that makes the buyer feel more comfortable in the purchase of the home. Little academic literature exists on the value of homes sold with home warranties. Industry-sponsored studies tend to support whatever position is favorable to the industry. So, it was no surprise to read the results of a 2014 study completed by home warranty company American Home Shield. According to its study, homes covered by protection plans, on average, spend nearly 11 fewer days on the market and sell for more than $2,300 higher than homes sold without a home warranty. In a press release for the study, Tim Meenan, the executive director of the Service Contract Industry Council, said, "Purchasing a home is a significant investment and can create tremendous anxiety. . . . Fortunately, the extra protection of a [home warranty] service contract can ease this apprehension."[6] Regardless of the data, the insight here is correct.

Buyers are rightly concerned about the knowledge imbalance when purchasing a home. Sellers usually know the property better than the buyers possibly could, and sharing information with the buyer helps reduce that imbalance and gives the buyer additional confidence in making their purchase. A home warranty can further reduce the risk to the buyer by shifting the cost of an expensive repair required right after moving into the house to the warranty company.

CONCLUSION

It's important to keep the buyer funnel in mind. Knowing the path they'll take to purchasing a home allows you to target them at each stage along the way. By the time you meet a buyer, they are well on their journey through the buyer funnel. So make sure that you've presented the property in the best light, have shared crucial information, and have differentiated your house from the competition even in the early stages. Although you might think reducing buyer risk happens toward the bottom of the funnel, you can start reinforcing trust from the beginning, starting with the listing.

SETTING THE
LIST PRICE

One of the most crucial factors in the home sale process is setting the listing price. Incorrect pricing means the seller loses out on value that could otherwise be in their pockets. Set too low a price, and you give value to the buyer that you could have kept. Set too high a price, and you will need additional time to sell the house, or it may not sell at all. Homes listed at too high a price usually require price cuts before they sell and eventually end up selling for a final price that is lower than an appropriately set initial listing price. Owners of homes sitting on the market also have to cover the holding costs during this period, such as mortgage and taxes. Setting a listing price either too low or too high is bad.

So, how do we get to the listing price that is just right? There is no perfect answer. Each house is unique, markets are continually evolving, and specific seller preferences make pricing a home an individual exercise. We have already discussed factors that contribute to home prices at the regional, neighborhood, and individual home levels. We also know that home values are imprecise and that the actual value of a home can only be known when an informed buyer completes the purchase for the specific home. We have outlined why and how home values should be considered in a range and how that range could be 5 percent or even 10 percent higher or lower than the typically expected price of a home. So, we have a good foundation of information, but we need to get more specific to be able to list a home. We need to get to the *just right price.*

Home prices can be estimated in multiple ways. Most real estate agents use the backward-looking comparables method. This method is effective at putting a home in an approximate price range but can be complicated by a lack of usable comparable homes in a rapidly appreciating or depreciating market. Automated valuation models (AVMs) provide an alternative perspective but can be plagued by poor data or large error ranges. One approach, discussed previously, is to combine estimated selling prices from a comparables analysis with those from AVMs. Using these two approaches will frequently provide a reasonably tight pricing range that a seller should have confidence in for selecting a specific selling price.

This still leaves us with the question of how to select the best price at which to market the home. We start with our narrow price range, but the specific number at which to list the house will depend on how we plan to negotiate and the preferences of the seller and agent.

Broadly speaking, there are three pricing strategies: the *round number* strategy, the *just below* strategy, and the *precise* strategy. Each strategy has pros and cons and, interestingly, people react predictably and differently to each of them. The listing price is an opening move in what is usually a multipart negotiation. This initial number sets into motion a somewhat predictable set of follow-on back-and-forth offers as the deal is negotiated.

According to the round number strategy, you simply pick a round number as the listing price. This number is usually rounded to the nearest $5,000 or $10,000 of the middle of your calculated range. While simple to establish, this pricing strategy invites negotiation. Listing at a round number provides buyers with a mentally simple value to process and is the result of imprecision in the seller's analysis. Buyers sense this uncertainty and work to take advantage of it by offering a lower price for the home. For the seller, this is an acceptable initial offer, because they were not as set on the initial price as someone listing with a precise price, and the round number seller is willing to negotiate to a successful resolution. Because of the simplicity of a round number, sellers listing with this price signal that they are easier to work with and would be helpful through the due diligence and other parts of the post-contract period prior to closing.

In choosing the just below strategy, you will set your price "just below" a round number. You will typically also make the last nonzero digit either a nine or a four, such as $169,000 or $524,000. Although these may look like odd numbers, you may also find this strategy familiar. It is also known as *psychological pricing* or *charm pricing* and is used commonly in retail due to its proven effectiveness at increasing retailer profits. Buyers tend to view the price as lower than it actually is.[1] For example, $169,000 will seem closer to $160,000 than to $170,000 despite the reality.

This pricing strategy also invites negotiation, as buyers believe they have more flexibility with it. Buyers perceive—usually accurately—that the sellers have raised their price to a higher just below price with the intent of negotiating down to their target sales price. For buyers, the just below price signals that they should submit a low initial offer and then plan to respond to a higher counteroffer.

The precise pricing strategy includes numbers that are neither round nor charm prices and that, because of their opaque reasoning, have the appearance of being set through a detailed process. (Remember, your price range *will* be set through a detailed process; these strategies are specifically for the actual listing price.) Precise pricing can be further divided into low and high precise strategies by selecting a price slightly below a just below price or slightly above a round number price, respectively.

Buyers perceive a precise home price to be a well-developed price, informed by research and calculations, and they tend to respond to a precise price with an initial offer closer to the listing price as compared to the other two strategies. At the same time, these buyers perceive the seller to be more difficult, someone who, in addition to asking for close to a full price, is going to be equally difficult during both the offer negotiations and when discussing home repairs and other items discovered during due diligence or who, in the words of one agent, is "someone who's going to argue about leaving a curtain rod."[2]

Which of these strategies is best? That depends on how you define what your best outcome is. Some sellers may value a sales price close to their list price. Others, such as those trying to maximize their sales price, would define the best outcome as the highest price realized. Understandably, researchers have been asking the same question.

In one study by researchers Eric Cardella of Texas Tech University and Michael Seiler of William & Mary, potential buyers and sellers participated in a simulated negotiation.[3] The researchers designed the negotiation scenario to be the same for all participants, with the exception of the list price. The subsequent negotiation process, including counteroffers, was observed and recorded.

The study generated several insights, starting with the observation that the listing price strategy does affect negotiations. The chosen strategy has implications for follow-on negotiations and, eventually, for the agreed upon contracted price. The results of the experiment showed that the precise strategy, and specifically the high precise strategy, resulted in the highest final price and the smallest discount to list price, while the just below strategy tended to lead to the lowest final price and the largest discount. So, one vote for the high precise strategy.

In a different study, Eli Beracha of Florida International University and Michael Seiler also looked at actual sales data of several hundred thousand transactions in the Hampton Roads, Virginia, region. After making adjustments to be able to compare home sales, the researchers found similar results.[4] This time, the worst strategy for a seller was the round number strategy, and the just below strategy performed the best. Although the just below strategy led to the largest discounts, the houses were overpriced to such a degree—including by over 5 percent in some cases—that they accommodated the discount, and the sellers were still able to come out ahead. The precise price strategy showed better results than the round number strategy but underperformed compared with the just below strategy. This analysis did not differentiate between a high and low precise strategy. Here, the just below strategy was best, but the high precise and low precise were not broken out. So, one vote for the just below strategy but with high precise still being a valid approach.

In their 2015 book *Zillow Talk*, Zillow co-founder Spencer Rascoff and Zillow chief analytics officer Stan Humphries looked at the same pricing strategies from a different angle. They compared homes' final sales price to their expected values for those homes listed using the round number strategy and those listed with a just below strategy or, more specifically, homes whose last nonzero digit was a nine (e.g., $199,000 or $349,000). They found that homes listed with a nine as the last nonzero digit consistently sold for prices 0.5 percent to 1.5 percent higher than those offered at round numbers.[5] This small difference translated to a realized selling price thousands of dollars higher than using a round number pricing. Another vote here for the just below strategy.

One practical observation found in several studies is how the initial listing price affects the negotiation behavior of both the buyer and the seller. Each of the three pricing strategies influences both a buyer's initial offer and a seller's counteroffer. Every seller has a target price in mind and sets their listing price with the intent of receiving that target as the final sales price. For most sellers, interestingly, this number is likely a round number. Round numbers are easy to process mentally and are usually only a small amount away from wherever the list minus negotiation price is likely to end. A seller is more likely to expect to take home $520,000 rather than $519,000 or $521,200, even though those values vary by less than 0.25 percent. The concept of a price range for a home continues to apply here, and home sellers know prices can be "squishy" and imprecise.

The perceptions of buyers and sellers, though, may not completely reflect what is actually happening. According to research by a team of academics from Cornell University and Indiana University, there are mechanisms at work when evaluating a low price.[6] One is a low-price signal, meaning the precise price would indicate the seller is cost-conscious and has deliberately lowered the price as much as they can to get to the precise price listed. The second is the expected negotiability mechanism, which I described earlier; this mechanism assumes that the precise price signals to the buyer that the seller would be difficult to negotiate with. A third mechanism is what these researchers refer to as the *learned precision-magnitude association* hypothesis. This hypothesis indicates that humans generally think in small numbers and use rounding as a mechanism for thinking in larger numbers. This mental shortcut is one reason why humans believe the difference between 1 and 2 is larger than the difference between 99 and 100, despite the difference being exactly the same. The learned precision-magnitude association would cause the appearance of a price such as $424,855 to seem much lower than a home priced nearly the same at $425,000 despite the nominal difference of only $145.

In their analysis of 27,000 home sales, the researchers found a link between more-precise list pricing and higher total sales price. In one sample looking at house prices in Florida, the calculations showed that more-precise home prices, whose last digits were rounded to three zeros (e.g., $425,000) had selling prices 0.72 percent lower than homes with list prices ending with two zeros (e.g., $424,700). The effect continued to homes with list prices ending with four zeros (e.g., $450,000). The additional zero in the price correlated with a selling price relatively lower than homes priced with three zeros or two zeros.

Using this approach, despite the small percentage impact, could be worth several hundred or even several thousand dollars to the seller. The relationship between more-precise list pricing and higher sales price held up across the other region studied and accounting for other potential variables. This study is another vote for using precise pricing. While the study results did not indicate a clear winning strategy, the precise strategy and the just below strategy both appear to result in homeowners selling their homes for higher prices than the round number strategy does.

The science of determining optimal listing price strategies is not settled, and there are counterarguments to the absolute best strategy. As one example countering the suboptimal value of a round number strategy, some experts recommend setting a price at a website search bracket breakpoint, such as $200,000, with the thought being that your home would show up in a search of homes with the lowest price of $200,000 and another set of searches with $200,000 at the highest end. A price of $199,000, for example, would not show up in a search for homes between $200,000 and $250,000. Because buying patterns are shifting more to online searches, shopping behavior will change, and further research will be necessary to understand how people respond to various listing strategies in the future.

Given what we know, what strategy should we as a seller use? The answer is . . . it depends. The field of behavioral economics is rapidly evolving. There are likely to be many reasons people respond to initial list prices in a certain way, and understanding this behavior will almost certainly be an area of future studies. As this knowledge improves, we can expect the findings to inform how home sellers choose which listing price strategy best meets their needs to complete the sale.

The round number strategy is mentally easy but seems to lose in just about any comparison of final sales price with the other strategies. There is some support for the idea that fewer syllables in the pronunciation of a sales price can make expensive items appear less pricey (e.g., an item priced at $200—pronounced "two hun-dred" using only three syllables—sounds less expensive than a price with more verbal syllables such as the seven syllables in $197), but the data at this point is inconclusive at best.

Since the available data points toward the high precise strategy, I recommend using that strategy if you are comfortable with being somewhat unconventional. For a more traditional approach, using the time-tested and often-used just below strategy is not a bad way to go. You could even consider increasing the precision of the just below method by ending a price with 900 rather than 000 (e.g., $379,900 instead of $379,000). Regardless of the approach chosen, you should understand that the listing price you choose will impact the buyer's perception of the home and will influence their initial offer price.

DEVELOPING AN EFFECTIVE LISTING

Now that we have our initial listing price established, our next step to selling a home for its full value is to create an effective listing. The listing is a crucial piece of marketing a property. And like any other sort of marketing, there can be good and bad listings. We will walk through what those look like and how to ensure your listing speaks to the best ready, willing, and able buyer for your home.

Today, most home buyers begin their search online,[1] and nearly half of all home buyers and the majority of buyers under the age of 50 have found the house they purchased online.[2] And similar to how most buyers move through the sales funnel in a predictable way, most buyers tend to view websites in a certain predictable way. This pre-dictability allows smart sellers to anticipate the buyer's thoughts and develop a listing that shows exactly what buyers expect to see.

Technology helps us understand this in detail. One such technology is ocular tracking, which researchers use to observe exactly where a subject's eye is looking on an image or a screen. The technology follows the user's view as they look at images. These trackers also capture the amount of time a viewer looks at an image, which points within the image they focused on, how long they focused on those different points, and the distance between the focal points. Examples of focal areas on a webpage could be a person's face, a call to action badge, or a shiny object, such as an engagement ring.

For online marketers, how viewers see their advertisements is crucial information. These experts often conduct what is known as *A/B testing* to determine which of two versions is more effective at converting views into sales. Simple differences, such as moving call to action buttons or certain images, can dramatically change the effectiveness of an advertisement. As an example, take two versions of a website with a photo of a baby on the left side. Version A has a photo of the baby facing to the front, toward the viewer, on one half of the screen, with additional text and images showing baby products for sale on the right. Version B has the baby facing sideways, toward the text on the right. Ocular tracking of viewers would show that nearly everyone would look directly at the baby's face in version A, because it is human nature to look directly at faces—especially baby faces. Few viewers of version A would move their eyes toward the actual ad copy, in contrast to version B, where the baby facing the ad copy leads most viewers to look first at the baby, then follow the baby's gaze to the copy. For advertisers, version B would be many times more effective than version A. The science here is well developed, and professional advertisers are able to leverage our natural human instincts to maximize sales of their products. Just as professional marketers work diligently to create the most effective advertisements for their products, so should home sellers.

Fortunately, we do not have to test different formats across hundreds of viewers of a property. We can take advantage of previous analyses, which can guide us in developing a better listing. The large number of transactions in the residential real estate market and the increasing use of online sites by buyers provided researchers at Old Dominion University in Virginia the opportunity to answer the question of how exactly online viewers look at home sale listings. Using ocular tracking technology, the researchers tracked users as they viewed online home listings to determine how they absorbed information and what was most important to the viewers.[3]

The researchers identified a clear and consistent viewing pattern across all of the experiment's participants as they looked at potential homes. This pattern consisted of four steps, although not all viewers would go through each step for each home. If the viewers were no longer interested in a home at any step along the way, they simply stopped looking at the current house and moved on to the next. This pattern starts with buyers looking at the photo of the exterior of the home. This is usually the first photo in a listing by convention and what most buyers look for initially. Next, the buyers scanned through other photos of the home, with no apparent prioritization. There was no trend indicating the buyers spent more time looking at, for example, the kitchen or the bathroom. As a third step, the buyers viewed the quantitative information about the home, such as the price, the number of bedrooms, the number of bathrooms, and the square footage. Finally, if the buyers made it to that point, they read the agent's written remarks about the home. In the study, only about 20 percent of the home buyers actually read the written description. For most buyers, looking at the photos along with the price and size of the house was enough information to determine whether to spend additional time looking at the listing.

The Old Dominion study's findings align well with real experience. Home listings that show the interior first are usually hiding the fact that the exterior of the home is unappealing (remember the value of curb appeal). The viewing pattern also aligns well with how buyers screen properties. The homes have already passed an initial search filter on location, price, and number of bedrooms and are now being compared with other homes that meet the same screening criteria. The buyers are making trade-offs using the information available.

For home sellers, the listing photos, the price, and the description are the keys for buyers to keep the homes in their funnels. Curb appeal and a clean and decluttered home continue their importance to the listing process, as the exterior photo and additional interior photos are key factors in appealing to buyers.

LISTING PHOTOS

We now know buyers tend to start by looking at the exterior curb appeal photo and then view the other photos. The quantity and quality of these photos do matter and influence whether the house is visited and how much the buyer is willing to offer for the home.

Quantity is straightforward: According to an analysis conducted by Zillow, the just right number is somewhere between 16 and 21 photos.[4] Having fewer than nine photos increases the risk of the home taking longer to sell.

Photo quality is a less obvious attribute but has been proven to have a tangible impact on a home's selling price. Professional photography has been shown to help sell a home faster and, in most cases, sell for thousands of dollars more than listings with simply average photos. Redfin compared the final sales price and the time on market for listings with professionally taken photos with those with amateur photos.[5] It found that, for homes priced between $200,000 and $1 million, those with professional photos sold for 1 percent to 2 percent more than those with amateur photos. This increase translates into an additional $3,000 to $11,000 for the seller. These homes also sold faster, on average, than comparable homes with only amateur photography. Considering that the cost of professional home photography is in the range of a couple hundred dollars, not having a home professionally photographed would be a mistake for nearly all homeowners looking to maximize their sales prices.

When we sold our townhome in Raleigh, we had the home photographed by professionals, who did an excellent job. They applied their skills by choosing the best angles to make the rooms appear as large in the photos as the space was in real life. They also adjusted the lighting of each room, chose a day with good natural light, and used higher-quality equipment than the average home seller has access to. Their work helped to make the house show online the best it possibly could.

Figure 8.1. Exterior photo of the Raleigh townhome

Figure 8.2. Interior photo of the Raleigh townhome

Interestingly, our competition at the time was another townhome across the street. In many ways it was superior to ours: It was built around the same time but had more square footage and an open backyard much larger than ours. Fortunately for us, though, the photos of the competing house were terrible. They were blurry, dark, and incomplete. The result was that the house was on the market for months, whereas ours sold right away. High-quality, professional photographs make a strong, positive first impression, especially online.

THE POWER OF WORDS

Just as high-quality, professional photography makes a difference in how homes are marketed and how much they can sell for, words in the listing description can be influential. Remember, buyers who take the time to read the home's written description have determined the property fits their initial broad criteria, the photos have kept their interest, and the basic numerical information, such as price and the number of rooms, are within the range they would consider purchasing. To further entice these potential buyers, sellers writing a description of their home should choose their words wisely, because the right wording could result in a quicker sale at a higher price. The opposite is also true; choosing less-flattering words could signal the house to be less than desirable, turning away potential buyers, and could mean the home takes longer to sell at a lower price.

The large number of online real estate information companies and the vast amount of data they collect and analyze helps us to understand what works and what does not in the listing description. Like any professional marketer, these companies have evaluated thousands of individual data points and identified relationships between elements of the listing and a sales price relative to the expected value or comparable home sale values. The use of certain words can impact potential buyers in subtle ways and can impact the associated sales price positively or negatively.

In their book *Zillow Talk*, Zillow co-founder Spencer Rascoff and chief analytics officer Stan Humphries highlight several relationships between listing length, wording, and other characteristics.

According to Rascoff and Humphries, listings with longer descriptions tend to sell for more than expected.[6] The opposite is also true. The shorter a listing description, the less a home sells for. There are limits to this relationship, but the optimal listing length is somewhere in the range of 50–75 words for a solid listing description. From a technical data-entry perspective, there are limits to how long a listing description can be. As an example, the Raleigh–Durham-area MLS allows 510 characters for remarks on a property. A listing of 50–75 words would take full advantage of the space the system allows.

The selection of words used in the description is also crucial. In another analysis, Rascoff and Humphries evaluated several adjectives in listings and compared those with the square footage of the home being described.[7] Rascoff and Humphries tested to see whether key words that subtly indicate a small home, such as *cute, quaint,* and *charming,* are actually associated with smaller homes. As the authors expected, the data supported their hypothesis. Homes with the word *cute* in the listing description generally had about two-thirds of the square footage of the homes they were being compared with.

This insight intuitively makes sense but is also a caution for agents or others who draft listing descriptions that include these sorts of words. There is no need to make a house sound smaller than it actually is when most home buyers seek a larger home for the price they are willing to pay. Buyers can make their own determination of a home's value to them given its size.

It's best to avoid terms that might imply a small size, advanced age, or low quality. For example, attributes of low-end homes, such as *investor, cosmetic,* and *TLC,* in the descriptions of high-end homes could lower the sales prices by 6 percent to 9 percent. Similarly, buyers expect a mid-tier home to be in good condition, without significant work required after the purchase. These buyers can read through certain words to understand what the listing description really means. Words like *nice, cosmetic,* and *bargain* are unattractive. They signal either a lack of attractive features or indicate that significant work will be required to upgrade the home. Negative words, such as *TLC, potential,* and *investment,* can lower the expected sales price of even low-end homes by up to 6 percent.[8] The word *fixer* should certainly be avoided, if possible; according to Rascoff and Humphries, this word could reduce the sales price relative to the expected price by more than 10 percent.

A well-written description should highlight what differentiates the home from others with similar prices, the same number of rooms, and similarities in other basic criteria. Broadly speaking, there are three general categories of homes ranked by quality: high-end, mid-tier, and low-end. High-end homes feature a high level of workmanship and high-grade materials throughout the interior and exterior of the home. High-grade materials and finishes could mean thick crown molding in most rooms, granite countertops, solid hardwood floors, custom closets, and other finishes upgraded from the builder's stock. Low-end homes typically feature economy and basic functionality as the primary considerations. These homes have little interior and exterior detail and are constructed with inexpensive stock materials and few or no upgrades. These structures meet the minimum building codes but provide few extras. Mid-tier homes, by definition, sit between these two levels and tend to balance affordability and luxury. These homes exceed acceptable building standards, and the finishes include a mix of both stock and high-quality materials. These might include soft-touch-closing drawers, especially in the kitchen; stainless steel appliances; or hardwood flooring.

When you're writing a listing description, the best differentiators are those that make the home comparable to the next level of aspirational homes. Attributes more typically found in mid-tier homes would be a differentiator in low-tier homes, and high-end features would stand out in mid-tier homes. Highlighting what makes these homes different from similar homes helps to increase buyer interest, and because the buyer demand is higher, it ultimately helps to sell the home for a higher price. However, we must be careful as we write these descriptions. The crucial piece to understand is how to highlight those elements that are aspirational to next-level homes. Highlighting lower-level attributes could actually hurt the sales price of the home; buyers would assume the house to be more similar to a lower-tier home.

As one example, Rascoff and Humphries looked at listings with the word *granite*. Granite surfaces are more typical in mid-tier and high-end homes than in low-end homes. Rascoff and Humphries observed low-end homes selling for over 4 percent more than the otherwise expected selling price when their listing mentioned granite.[9] However, in mid-tier homes, where granite seems less rare, homes whose listings mentioned it sold for less than 3 percent over the expected price. The impact in high-end homes is even less, because this sort of high-quality feature would be expected; it does not significantly differentiate the home from its comps. These homes sold for only 1 percent over the expected selling price, so you can see that even though the difference was smaller, mentioning granite surfaces did help raise the value over homes that did not mention it. Other listing words that lifted sales prices included *stainless*, *remodel*, and *landscaped*. Each of these words added between 1 percent and 4 percent of the sales price, with the greatest lift in the lower-tier homes.

For a $300,000 home, this small percentage is actually an impact of $3,000–$12,000. For more expensive homes, the impact is even greater. If you employ a real estate agent, whose commission is generally in the range of 4 percent to 6 percent of the price of the home, writing an effective description can create enough value to offset their entire cost.

Low-end home buyers tend to highly value selected upgrades that are more commonly found in mid-tier and high-end homes. Words that indicate amenities, such as *luxurious*, *impeccable*, *spotless*, and *tile*, all contribute to a low-end home selling at a price higher than the typically expected sales price.

There is skill in writing a listing to attract the right buyers. Let's look at a few listing descriptions examples for a mid-tier home. Each has been modified from actual listing descriptions.

This three-story home has granite countertops in
the kitchen and master bath, hardwood flooring,
a tankless water heater, a fireplace, and a two-car
garage. Upgraded features include updated interior
paint and new carpet in some rooms.

At 36 words and 235 characters, this description is short and high-lights features I would expect in a mid-tier home. The tankless water heater is a positive feature but would be low on any buyer's aspirational wish list. (Can you hear the buyers talking after their home visit? "This home is amazing. It has a tankless water heater!") This is not the best-written description.

MOVE IN READY! New Carpet & Hardwoods! Large
back screened porch w/ private backyard. Kitchen
features stainless steel appliances, ample cabin-
etry, recessed lighting, double ovens & breakfast
area. Separate dining & living rooms. Dual staircase
& walk up attic. Oversize Master bedroom offers
a ceiling fan & privacy bath. Master bath includes
dual sinks, separate shower & garden tub. All
bedrooms have ceiling fans & good size closets. A
MUST SEE!

This description has 71 words and 449 characters, which is better than the previous example. But, other than the private backyard, I have trouble understanding what is aspirational about most of the attributes mentioned; this is not an exciting description even though it wants you to think so with the all caps and exclamation marks.

Interestingly, the photos of the home showed granite counters in the kitchen, a well-built screened-in porch, a finished third floor, and a whirlpool bathtub upstairs. The tub would correctly date the home to the mid-1990s but is an opportunity to differentiate from competing homes. The house looked to be in excellent condition and was spotless on the inside. The house is also in a good location convenient to several amenities in the surrounding area. By not mentioning these differentiators, the description does not do a great job selling the home to a potential buyer who has shown enough interest to read the description.

> Go green! Stylish Charleston-style home close to shops. Leave the car and take the greenway to school and the sidewalk to the green grocer. Gain renewed energy from flexible spaces and plantation shutters, granite kitchen and bathrooms, stainless steel appliances and elegant moldings. Enjoy your daily greens in the kitchen open to family room. The grass is actually greener from the deck with a pergola and rear fenced garden.

At 69 words and 428 characters, the length of this last example allows potential buyers to get a sense of the home. The description focuses extensively on differentiators, such as the house style, its location, and the unique garden and lot while covering some of the nice-to-have features of granite, stainless steel, and moldings. The description is speaking to a unique buyer and highlighting many of the attributes not readily apparent by looking at the photos and the basic house information. This is an example of an excellent listing description.

Our mid-tier Raleigh townhome was marketed with what I believe to be a pretty good description:

> Beautiful, conveniently located and well-maintained end unit townhouse! Master features walk-in closet, dual sinks and garden tub/shower combo; second bedroom also has en-suite bathroom. SS appliances, open floor plan, crown molding, large bonus that could be used as third bedroom and private back deck. This is a newer townhome unit with fiber cement siding and is an energy-efficient home in a prime location! This home will not last long, please bring forth your highest and best offer!

Here, the writer focused on a few of the differentiators, such as crown molding, the unique bonus room, the age of the home, and the location. Combined with the excellent photographs, the professionally written listing successfully differentiated the townhome. The quality of the listing was confirmed by the results: a quick sale at a good price for the seller.

Although you must be honest about what you or your agent writes in the description, you also must be aware of the potential target buyer, their attributes, and the impact of certain words that might influence their buying decision. The choice of words can affect the speed of the sale and, done well, can increase the sales price of the home by 5 percent to 10 percent.

PUTTING IT TOGETHER

A quality listing is a key element in selling a home for its full value. Today's home buyers increasingly look for homes online, so the online listing can make or break a sale. A quality listing can sell a home in days, whereas a poor one may take weeks or months in the same market. Thanks to academic research, we know how buyers think when looking at homes, and we can be one step ahead of them by meeting their expectations with every click from the first photo to the detailed wording in the listing description.

Creating an effective listing is a must-do for home sellers and their agents, but unfortunately, surprisingly few listings are well crafted. The keys to a quality listing are simple: Use professional photography, include a sufficient number of photos, show the home's exterior in the first listing photo, choose aspirational words in the listing, and do not simply list what the buyers already know. Taking these actions is not difficult, costs virtually nothing, and can lead to a higher selling price for your home.

TIMING: WHEN TO MARKET

When it comes to selling a house, timing matters. Houses listed at more optimal times of the year can sell quicker and for more money. For those flexible in when they can sell, there is usually a better time of year to put their home on the market relative to other times, and the day of the week the listing goes live is also important. Again, knowing the predictable patterns of buyers can be used to the seller's benefit.

Residential real estate is a seasonal business. Although it varies by specific geography, across most of the United States, sales start slowly at the beginning of the year as the winter months of January and February dissuade buyers from eagerly looking at homes. Homes on the market during this period also do not tend to show as well, because the days are short, trees are barren, and the yard is dull or covered in snow. However, homes do start to hit the market as sellers who were holding off for the end-of-year holidays are now seeking to list their homes. By March or April, buyers are starting to look more, and more sellers are considering selling their homes. The end of the school year is coming up quickly, and people are looking to both sell and buy in this period to make their moves during the summer months. March and April also feature more comfortable weather, and people are generally in a positive mood after a dark and cold winter season. May starts the beginning of the selling season in much of the country. Home sales typically peak in the months between the school year—May, June, July, and August. Once the summer winds down in September, so do house sales, with further declines in sales through the holiday months of November and December. The end of the year—specifically December—tends to be the worst time to list a home and should be avoided if at all possible by the seller.

Not all regions follow this trend. Vacation destinations, such as Florida beach towns, can see increased sales during the peak tourist seasons, which could be in the winter. Warmer geographic regions, again such as Florida beach towns, may see lower sales volume in the hot summer months as the weather makes visiting homes less enjoyable. University towns have their own special cycles and sometimes experience increased sales of rental apartments in the shoulder seasons of late spring and early fall as graduate students and professors look for places to stay and parents purchase investment properties for their children to reside in for the next several years (and the parents can deduct the cost of visiting their kids in college!).

For sellers, listing at the optimal time can be worth thousands of dollars. Zillow, in another of its research studies, calculated that, in the United States, listing in early May would realize an average premium of 1.2 percent, or about $2,400, and would result in a sale nearly 13.5 days faster than homes listed in other months.[1] This data point comes with a number of caveats; again, the optimal time of year to list varies by region and the specific market conditions in those areas at that time.

CHOOSE THE DAY

Choosing which day to list can also impact the initial demand for a home. Going back to our buyer funnel, we know that interested buyers will want to quickly visit any homes that compare favorably with other homes on their list. We also know that most buyers tend to have commitments during the workweek and will research homes during the week but plan to visit them on the weekend. By listing toward the end of the week—on a Thursday, Friday, or Saturday— you are able to tap into the buyer's interest. Homes listed on these days tend to sell for a premium and faster than homes listed on other days of the week.

When we sold our Raleigh townhome, we chose to list it on Thursday, which did actually create significant interest. We then held an open house that Saturday—two days later. This led to interested buyers visiting in good numbers.

Optimally timing when to list is another small but subtle action to increase the speed and price of a home sale. As a seller, you want to meet the needs of the best ready, willing, and able buyer by listing when they are looking.

THE CRUCIAL FIRST 14 DAYS

Interest in most homes peaks in the first 14 days after listing, so it is important for sellers to time their listing to capture as much interest as possible early on. Sellers can also expect to realize a higher selling price if the home goes under contract within 14 days. After 14 days, the listing becomes stale as newer, fresher listings come to the market.

This makes sense if we understand the buyer's behavior. Buyers working through the buyer funnel will continuously search for newly listed homes that meet their criteria. As these homes hit the market, the buyers will quickly evaluate these homes as a potential match for their needs. If the home is a match, they will move quickly to visit and submit an offer on the home. If there is no match, they will continue to wait for additional homes to be listed or will begin to adjust their criteria to find a home that meets most of their preferences. After 14 days, your property is less likely to show up in the buyer's search. Even if their changed criteria match your home, there are two weeks of newer properties that will appear above yours in the search results.

To put some numbers behind this insight, Zillow examined listing interest for homes in the days following listing. The company found that listing interest, calculated as the median number of daily listing views on its website, was highest on the first day after listing and then rapidly dropped off. As an example, at the national level, homes would have a median of 82 views on the first day, 48 the second day, 41 on the third day. This number would continue to decline to 18 views per day after 14 days and would continue its slow decline in interest beyond.[2]

This rapid decline in buyer interest after listing correlates with a lower selling price. In a different analysis, Zillow calculated the difference in sales price from list price compared with time on the market. In its results at the national level, Zillow found sales prices to be within 2 percent of the list price for homes selling within two weeks and then a continuous decline in price the longer the home was on the market. In this analysis, homes on the market for 80 days would sell for 6 percent less than the list price.[3]

Home sale patterns vary by geography, price range, market cycle, and other factors, but the overall insight is clear: Buyer interest is highest in the first 14 days after listing. After that, the likelihood of selling at a greater discount to the initial listing price increases. As a seller, you should be prepared to take advantage of this interest and maximize selling opportunities in this window. Practically speaking, this would mean hosting an open house on the first weekend the home is on the market to allow buyers to visit the home without having to formally organize a visit through an agent. Conventional wisdom is for agents to host open houses later in the process to drum up interest in the home—and business for themselves—but, in reality, buyer interest will have already flattened by then.

Again, in selling our Raleigh townhome, we were able to maximize buyer interest in the first weekend by holding an open house the Saturday after our Thursday listing. As was expected, with an open house less than 48 hours after listing, we had many potential buyers viewing the house, which resulted in multiple offers the next day. We successfully worked within the buyer's house-searching process, accelerated the visit phase, and received offers in the process.

SELECTING A GOOD AGENT

Many sellers ask themselves whether they should hire a real estate agent, and if so, which one. Most will hire an agent; selecting the right one is more difficult. The market is crowded with many different agents advertising their services everywhere you look. Many sellers default to using either a friend or a friend's friend, choosing an unknown agent they may have met while searching for homes, or—if they are lucky—using an agent they used for a previous transaction. More precisely, 41 percent of sellers found their agent through a referral by a friend, neighbor, or relative; another 12 percent used an agent they had used before; and the remainder found their agent through other means, such as visiting an agent's website, receiving a direct mail piece, or walking into a real estate agency, according to research by the National Association of Realtors.[1]

None of these methods relates to how well the agents perform their jobs. There is a level of knowledge, skill, experience, and professionalism required to be what we would consider a professional real estate agent. These agents have both the hard knowledge and the soft skills to successfully complete a transaction to the best interest of their clients. Hard knowledge in the industry includes an in-depth understanding of the home buying and selling process, knowledge of home types, detailed understanding of the current market specific to the property, knowledge of negotiation principles, and fluent knowledge of the content of the relevant contracts. An agent's soft skills would include understanding their clients' needs and preferences, communicating in an appropriate and responsible manner, and conducting every action in a professional manner.

Real estate is a highly regulated space. This governmental control is intended to protect consumers from incompetent or criminal real estate agents. The potential impact of a bad transaction is large, with many contributing factors. Nearly every state tightly manages the process of how real estate agents earn licenses and how they operate with those licenses. States also have strict processes and laws detailing the requirements of how residential homes are sold, which can include consumer protections such as mandatory disclosures. The states' requirements help manage the minimum competencies for real estate agent license holders but do not guarantee them to be a highly competent, professional agent.

"What do you call the medical student who graduates at the bottom of their class? Doctor." The same is true for real estate agents. Not all agents are experts in buying and selling real estate. Licensed agents know the basics of buying and selling real estate and how to stay out of trouble with the state regulatory bodies, but of the total population of licensed real estate agents, relatively few perform as true professionals.

Despite the wide range of agent skills, total agent commission has remained in an unusually tight range—around 5 percent to 6 percent, regardless of the skill, services provided, or the price of the home being sold. Agents listing homes do not usually take home this amount of commission. Roughly half will be shared with the agent representing the buyer, with the listing agent keeping the remainder.

Although a 5 percent to 6 percent commission is considered fairly typical in the United States, this amount is nearly twice what agents charge in Europe. Commissions of approximately 1 percent to 3 percent are common in the United Kingdom,[2] and 2 percent is considered normal in the Netherlands.[3] The average American real estate agent also tends to complete fewer transactions each year relative to their European counterparts: A typical American agent tends to close between 5 and 10 transactions annually; British agents close closer to 40. This disparity has been a topic of discussion in many articles, with no clear explanation emerging. One outcome of the result, however, is that American agents spend a disproportionate amount of time on sourcing and competing for buyer and seller leads.

A common refrain of American agents is that they are worth the cost of their commission. This value is determined by the needs of the seller or buyer and the contribution of the agent. In some cases, agents do provide value well beyond their costs—such as agents who advise their clients of the recommendations found in the previous chapters. In other cases, agents can fail to add value or potentially destroy value for their principals by advising sellers to sell too low or buyers to overpay for their homes.

Academics have struggled to determine whether agents add quantifiable value. Although the answer remains unclear, several academic studies tend to point toward a negative answer: Real estate agents do not add value to a sales transaction. Several data points support this answer. First, real estate agents are better informed than their clients, and some agents take advantage of this difference. Agents are compensated when a home sells, and since they earn only a small fraction of the selling price, they are incentivized to advise their clients to sell their homes at too low a price and too quickly. Agents benefit only a fraction more by selling a home at a higher price, but they completely bear the additional costs of managing more showings, hosting open houses, investing in additional marketing, and taking the time required to provide status updates to their clients. Taken to an extreme, rational agents would accept an immediate but relatively low offer to receive their commission rather than take the extra time and effort to achieve a better outcome for their client but at little additional benefit to themselves.[4]

Researchers at the University of Chicago looked into just this relationship. To test their hypothesis that agents do not always act in their client's best interest, the researchers looked at over 100,000 home sales in the Chicago area, including those in which the agents were identified as selling homes they owned themselves. After adjusting for different variables to make the comparisons valid, the researchers found that homes owned by real estate agents sell for 3.7 percent more and stay on the market an average of 9.5 days longer.[5] This supports the theory that agents sell their own homes differently than they do their clients' homes.

This intuitively makes sense from an agent's financial perspective.

Using a $300,000 house as an example, the total commission on the sale using a traditional 6 percent rate would be $18,000. Of this, about 50 percent, or $9,000, would go to the agent on the other side of the transaction. Of the remaining 50 percent, nearly $4,500 would go toward the agent's brokerage firm and other costs the agent would incur in the transaction, such as marketing, signage, photography, and so on. At the end, the agent would take home a roughly $4,500 commission from the sale of this home. If a low offer of, say, $280,000 was submitted for the same house, the agent would then take home $4,200, only $300 less than the full-price commission, but if accepted, the agent would be able to receive their commission sooner and with less risk than if the offer was rejected and both the seller and agent had to wait for another, hopefully better, offer. And in the other direction, the 3.7 percent higher amount that agents typically sell their own homes for—a sales price of $311,100—would net the agent only an additional $166.50 commission. However, this amount contrasts with an agent selling their own home: A 3.7 percent increase in selling price would result in an additional $11,100 for the agent as seller. Compared with a potential personal gain of $167, that $11,100 is much more significant to the agent as seller and worth the additional investment in time and cost.

In a different study, researchers from Stanford University and Texas A&M University found that an agent's ability to post properties on the multiple listing service (MLS) accounted for all of an agent's value and offset the value-destructive behaviors, such as selling for too low of a price.[6] This study looked at real estate sales in Stanford University's faculty staff housing (FSH) neighborhoods in Palo Alto and neighboring cities in California. These homes were unique in that, at the time of the study, they were not listed on the MLS but, rather, on an internal site with Stanford's FSH division. Buyers and sellers could choose to hire an agent, but the homes would still not be listed on the MLS. These homes were similar in construction and price to nearby homes outside of FSH neighborhoods, and the price difference of homes sold with and without agents could be readily compared to evaluate how agents' contributions such as marketing and negotiation influenced final selling prices without the benefit of listing on the MLS. The researchers pulled sales data for nearly three decades and compared the pricing for similar homes sold with an agent and without an agent, making adjustments to ensure the home sales were comparable. The results showed that homes sold with an agent *lowered* the typical selling price by 5.9 percent to 7.7 percent compared with homes sold without an agent. The researchers argued that the costs of using an agent without the MLS far outweigh the benefits of an agent's knowledge and expertise.

In a third study, MIT economists examined the structure of real estate commissions and the number of real estate agents entering the market in Boston over a 20-year period.[7] Using sophisticated economic modeling, the researchers determined that the optimal number of agents serving the Boston market was well below the actual number of agents in the market and that the agents in the market were attracted by the relatively high commission structure of 5 percent to 6 percent, which could be earned with relatively little work. The researchers estimated the optimal commission structure to be about 50 percent less; the 2 percent to 3 percent more commonly seen in the United Kingdom would result in about 40 percent fewer real estate agents and 73 percent more transactions per agent. This structure would increase efficiency, because the agents would spend more productive time transacting homes rather than chasing leads to sell houses.

As a counter to the questionable value of an agent, the National Association of Realtors and other groups vested in the interest of real estate agents continually market the value agents provide to buyers and sellers. These groups regularly publish reports to claim the usefulness of real estate agents. According to the National Association of Realtors, "The typical [for sale by owner] home sold for $200,000 compared to $265,500 for agent-assisted home sales."[8] At face value, it sounds as though an agent can sell a house for over 30 percent more than an owner without an agent, but this simple statistic hides the variation among the homes that comprise the overall average. Although the claim may be factually correct, the implicit insight that an agent will deliver a superior selling price is incorrect and very much uncertain.

So, why are real estate agents still used in 90 percent[9] of residential real estate transactions if they cost more and potentially lower the sales price of a home? First, agents have access to their local MLS and can post homes for sale in the system. National real estate websites access the homes listed on these databases and pull data directly from them. A home posted on the MLS is typically then shared on Zillow, Trulia, Redfin, Realtor.com, and numerous similar sites. This exposure is a key reason to hire an agent. Second, agents do provide specific knowledge on a complex process, saving owners time and hassle. Finally, buying or selling a home is a rare transaction and involves high stakes. Most people buy or sell real estate only a few times in their lifetime, and when they do, they are selling their home, not just a house. Significant dollars are at stake with each decision in the selling process, as well as the seller's personal feelings if a potential buyer says the furnishings are "hideous" or the wall colors are "out of style." An agent does not have a personal attachment to the home and will not let these comments impact the sales process.

So, when it comes to finding the best agent in your area, don't just hire any friend, relative, or neighbor with a real estate license. Start by asking two questions: *How many transactions have you done in the last 12 months?* And *what value do you provide me relative to other agents?* A professional agent will have completed well over a dozen transactions in the past year. Any fewer and you have either a new agent or a part-time agent. This alone may not preclude them from representing you well, but it at least raises the expectations for their answer to the second question. A professional agent should have a well-developed response to how they provide value.

A listing agent can provide unique value in four areas: valuation, listing, marketing, and negotiation. Valuation is getting the price right and choosing the best pricing strategy to meet the seller's goals. Listing is creating the quality listing described earlier. Marketing consists of adding the property to the MLS but also includes a well-timed open house and additional digital and paper media. A good agent should also be well versed in negotiating tactics. Anybody with a state-issued real estate license should be expected to have a certain level of competency to help people buy or sell real estate. It is up to you as the seller to determine whether any specific agent has the knowledge and skills to add value to the transaction and to help you benefit more than the cost of the agent's commission.

Hire a real estate agent for all of the reasons detailed previously, but do so with your eyes wide open. Know what an agent can and cannot do, and hire the best agent you can find. Be cautious when hiring a friend, relative, or neighbor; instead, choose an agent who is a professional in the field. Agents are expensive, but the good ones, like any other true professional, excel at their chosen craft and provide valuable advice and assistance when selling your home.

A NOTE ON iBUYERS

Home sellers today have the option to sell to an iBuyer. This is a relatively new development to the market and offers homeowners the opportunity to sell their homes at a date of their choosing and then walk away. iBuyers initially included companies such as Offerpad and Opendoor, but larger companies such as Zillow and Redfin have started to offer iBuying services as well.

The concept is simple. You submit your home information to an iBuyer, and it will provide you an offer for your home. You can choose which date to close on. After the sale, the iBuyer will clean the house; make any additional updates, such as replacing carpets; and then list the home. For some buyers, the value of the speed and certainty of the sale without having to deal with a real estate agent is an attractive value proposition.

It is also a value proposition that comes at a steep cost. From what I've seen, iBuyer offers tend to come in at the low side of a home's value and also come with an additional service fee around 7 percent. In essence, you are selling your home at a low price and with an agent's commission taken out.

This industry is rapidly evolving, and I would expect to see it continue into the future. Precursors to iBuyers have existed for decades, but with the convergence of more accurate automated valuation models, digital imaging, readily available capital, and a population more trusting of online sales, an iBuyer offering is now more feasible and trusted. iBuyers will serve a segment of homeowners who just want to sell their house without any hassle and who are willing to accept the lower financial return. iBuyers are not intended for sellers expecting to sell their homes for full value and maximum profit.

PART 4

CLOSING THE DEAL

The final stage of selling a home is agreeing to the terms of a deal with the ready, willing, and able buyer. At this point in the process, a buyer has decided they would like to purchase your home and has demonstrated this commitment by providing a contract outlining their offer and the associated terms and timing. As a seller, you now have an offer to consider, and you can choose to either accept the offer as it has been presented or, more likely, negotiate to improve the offer to your benefit. Value earned through the preparation and listing processes can easily be lost during negotiation. Understanding how to negotiate the offer terms will help you keep this hard-earned value.

Once the offer is accepted, the deal is not yet done. Most real estate contracts provide the buyer with some sort of due diligence period, a time where they can look at their potential purchase in more detail to ensure the house is worth what the buyers have offered to pay. A well-prepared house should yield no surprises to buyers, and this contract-to-close period should be effortless. But in the residential real estate market, this is rarely the case. An issue of some sort almost always arises, and you should proactively address potential issues and have a plan to respond to other issues that may come up prior to the property transferring ownership.

Signing the offer contract represents the high-value point of the selling process. At this point, you will have maximized the negotiation with the buyer and have agreed to terms and conditions. Any discussions after the offer signing but prior to the property closing will usually involve an expense for the property seller. Keeping what you have earned is the key part of this final process.

NEGOTIATION

In the negotiation process, value can be created or lost or can shift between parties in minutes. Successful negotiation is a key requirement if you want to capture the full value of your house. For many people, the few minutes spent negotiating a deal can represent the largest swings of potential value they will ever experience in such a short period of time. Several tens of thousands of dollars could easily be lost or gained within a couple of back-and-forths of a real estate negotiation.

A successful negotiation will require effort from you and your agent and can be divided into three broad phases. First, you must do your research. In a negotiation, the side with the most information often wins. After doing the research, you must then prepare for the negotiating process. Just as a professional athlete would watch game films to prepare for an upcoming opponent, you should prepare for upcoming negotiations with a strategy and an understanding of who will be sitting across the table from you. Finally, you and your agent will need to negotiate the terms of a deal, sign a document agreeing to the terms, and then proceed to close the deal with the buyer.

Before we delve into specific details of the real estate negotiation process, we should step back to consider how to approach negotiations in general. Negotiations take place every day, and nearly everyone is frequently involved in negotiations. Of course, high-stakes negotiations such as international treaties and multibillion-dollar commercial contracts are the obvious examples, but more mundane negotiations include job offers, buying a new car, and purchasing furniture. Even low-stakes events, such as deciding what to eat for dinner, can be a negotiation. Although the items being negotiated can range from global to incidental, the negotiation process is similar. All negotiations are about finding common ground, with the goal of reaching an agreement on some matter. If no outcome were potentially possible, there would be no negotiation. Both parties in a negotiation would like something that the other side is able to provide.

The outcomes of negotiations are important to the parties negotiating and to those they represent. Successful negotiating is a topic that has been well researched and publicized, precisely because of the magnitude of the stakes. Despite the vast amount of information readily available on how to negotiate, relatively little has been written on the specific topic of residential real estate negotiations. To a large extent, this lack of specificity makes sense, because the approach for how to negotiate a large commercial contract is essentially the same as the approach to negotiate a more modest residential real estate transaction. In both of these scenarios, timing is not crucial, but getting the contractual details right is.

Both knowledge and experience are helpful to negotiating a successful outcome. Knowledge includes understanding the science of negotiations and the psychology, physiology, and outcome-based insights related to a negotiation. Equally important, though, is the art of the negotiation, which includes understanding the people aspect. Knowing the science and practicing the art of negotiation will help transform an initial offer into a successful deal.

THREE KEY NEGOTIATION CONCEPTS

Three basic negotiating concepts are relevant to home sellers: the value of information; the importance of options and alternatives, including knowing when to walk away; and the psychology of gains versus losses.

The side with the most information in a negotiation usually has the best outcome. Having information allows you to propose terms that are favorable to your side but realistic for the opposing side to agree to—for example, understanding the dealer's true price for a car, a supplier's cost structure for a certain product, or a typical salary range for a job. In real estate, this information is a deep understanding of the specific market, the specifics of the house for sale, and the situation for the sale as it relates to the other party.

To successfully negotiate, you must have a well-defined point at which you will be willing to walk away. As a seller, this could be structured in a couple of different ways, but they form a collective lower limit. That lower limit could be offers of $300,000 cash, $325,000 with a loan and short due diligence period, or $330,000 with a loan and longer due diligence period. Alternatively, you could have another buyer lined up and not have to give in to new terms in an initial offer. Having multiple options works both ways, and both buyers and sellers can strengthen their negotiating power by developing multiple acceptable options. Buyers can have additional negotiating power if similar homes are available. If a buyer could purchase the apartment next door for less than the one you are offering, this could be a good alternative for the buyer should you not agree to their terms.

Not all deals are good deals, and sometimes the best option is to walk away. All negotiators should know what this point is and should be willing to let the deal go when their criteria are not met. For those who study negotiations, this walkaway point is sometimes known as a BATNA or the "best alternative to a negotiated agreement."[1] Having alternative options can strengthen a BATNA. Conversely, if the house is perfect and in a perfect location for the buyer, and there is no good alternative, then the buyer will have the weaker hand and, typically, will have to yield more to the seller's asks.

Behavioral economics has shown that people feel losses more intensely than they feel gains. The hurt of a loss can feel up to twice as bad as the joy from a gain of the same amount.[2] That is, most people feel that a loss of $1,000 hurts about twice as bad as a gain of $1,000 pleases them. As humans, this means that we prefer to avoid losses whenever possible. This dynamic is one reason houses tend to sell slower in down markets than would be rationally expected. In a down market, the sellers feel the loss of their home's value compared with if they had sold during an up market. Say a woman purchased a condo in Florida in 2000 for $100,000. In 2007, at the top of the market, her neighbors sold similar condos for $500,000. The woman later sold her condo in 2014 for $350,000, but she was not happy. The sting of her selling at a "loss" of $150,000 outweighed her actual financial gain of $250,000. Losses hurt, and the parties should incorporate this understanding into how their offers and counteroffers are crafted and should frame potential losses as gains for the other party.

The negotiation process

At a high level, there are three main phases to a successful negotiation. First is research. You want to be the side with the most information. Second is planning. You need to determine your approach for the negotiation, such as your first steps, your reservation points, and the tone for the discussions. Finally, you complete the negotiations and agree to an outcome favorable to your side—and, ideally, to both sides for a win-win deal.

Research provides an understanding of what a good deal would look like for each side. From a real estate seller's perspective, this would mean determining what you would consider a good deal and what you would consider a bad deal. A similar exercise would be developed from the buyer's side, and you should determine what that perspective is to arrive at a deal acceptable to both parties. What would the buyer think would be a good deal? Your research should include the price of the home and the price of similar homes on the market, the general market in which the house is being sold, and any information about the buyer and their motivations for buying the home. This can take the form of a letter from the buyer stating why they want to buy your home, information shared between your agent and the buyer's agent, or publicly available information about the buyer such as a job promotion.

By this point, you should have a solid understanding of the factors that influence the value of a home and the specific tactics used to set the listing price. Furthermore, you should have an in-depth understanding of which homes on the market are competing with your house and what price nearby comparable homes have recently sold for. This information provides a snapshot into the current market conditions.

Understanding market trends adds a dynamic context to the static view developed above. Real estate markets are cyclical and tend to shift from a buyer's market to a seller's market and back over periods of years. Knowing where the market is for the specific property being sold is a crucial component to developing an effective negotiation strategy.

Simply stated, a buyer's market is when the supply of homes exceeds the demand. At the other end of the spectrum, a seller's market is when the demand for homes exceeds the supply. A market is balanced when the market's supply matches the market's demand.

Historically, the market at large cycles like a pendulum from a buyer's market to a balanced market to a seller's market, and then back to a balanced market and a buyer's market. If you look at the US residential housing market from 2005 to 2008, you would say it was a seller's market. The market across much of the country was hot, as home financing was readily available and housing became a can't-lose investment. There were far more ready, willing, and able buyers than there were homes available to meet these buyers' needs. The market switched quickly with the economic downturn of late 2008 and early 2009. The housing market quickly went from a seller's market to a buyer's market. Many homeowners were unable to afford the large homes or the second and third homes they easily purchased in the run up to 2008, as the stock market declines and mass layoffs slammed household finances. Homes across the country were foreclosed on and created a massive amount of available homes for sale. This increased supply amid low demand further decreased prices and created a vicious cycle for the speculative homeowners and others who had purchased toward the peak of the market. The buyer's market of 2009–2011 was a once-in-a-generation opportunity for real estate investors to purchase quality homes at deeply discounted prices. In this postcrash period, investors and value-minded purchasers were a key set of buyers in the market.

We must also understand the different needs and wants for different buyers that can influence specific submarkets. Buyers for a $250,000 single-family home are different from buyers for a $1-million-plus home. Because of these differences, it is not only possible but entirely likely that the market for homes priced less than $250,000 could be in an extreme seller's market while homes at the $1-million-plus range are in a buyer's market—rarely selling and, when they do, at well below list.

Although a buyer's and a seller's market can't be identified by scientific methods, several indicators point toward what type of market exists for the specific property being sold:[3]

- The days on the market
- The months of available inventory
- The number of showings
- The ratio of the list price to the close price
- Market price appreciation

Days on the market

Properties sitting on the market for a greater number of days, on average, indicate more of a buyer's market. When the typical number of days on the market is in the single digits and stories abound of listings receiving multiple offers within hours of going active, a seller's market is likely in play.

Months of inventory

The amount of residential real estate inventory can be envisioned as water flowing in and out of a pond. Nearly all of the time, homes are available for sale, just as a pond contains a certain level of water. At the same time, additional homes are listed for sale while others are purchased, just as a freshwater pond has streams feeding into and out of it, continually replacing the water. To estimate the months of inventory supply, we take the number of homes available on the market in a particular period and divide that by the number of homes sold or contracted during the same period. In the pond analogy, the calculation would be the amount of time it would take for the pond to empty if no additional water replenished it over that time. Broadly speaking, less than five months of inventory would indicate a seller's market, more than seven is a buyer's market, and between five to seven months of inventory would be considered a neutral market.[4]

The number of showings

As we would expect, the number of showings for an appropriately priced property in good condition would indicate what type of market the property is in. In a seller's market, we would expect many showings, whereas in a buyer's market, the same property could have few to no showings. A good real estate agent should be able to provide information on the typical number of showings for a home to sell.

List-price-to-close ratio

The ratio of the list price to the closing price is another indicator of where the market is. If most homes are selling at near or over 100 percent of their list price, the market would be considered a seller's market. On the other hand, if the list-to-close ratios approach 90 percent, those figures would indicate a buyer's market.

Market price appreciation

As we discussed earlier, if the demand for homes exceeds the supply, we expect prices to rise and the homes in that market to appreciate. This market appreciation is an indicator of the current housing market. If appreciation is above 5 percent annually, the market would be considered a seller's market. If prices are flat or declining year over year, then that indicates a buyer's market.

Each of these five metrics is a guideline, and there are nuances to how each is calculated, but as a group, the indicators should give a reasonably clear view of whether the current market for the specific property is a seller's, buyer's, or balanced market.

Knowing the current market conditions is a key to understanding how to negotiate during the offer process. In a strong seller's market, an appropriately priced home in good condition would be expected to elicit multiple offers in just a few days. In a buyer's market, the same house could be expected to yield one offer in several weeks. Knowing the market will influence not only your aggressiveness in the selling price but also your expectations for negotiation in areas such as the form of purchase financing (e.g., cash versus a more burdensome type of payment) and completing buyer repair requests.

Finally, to prepare for any negotiation, the seller should do their best to understand who exactly will be across the negotiation table. Once you have a contract with potential buyers, you should aim to understand their motives and negotiation levers. You would approach negotiating with a young nurse looking to purchase her first home at the lowest possible price differently from how you would deal with a dual-lawyer couple looking to buy a house for their in-laws, in which price is not a major factor, and this would be different still from negotiating with a financial buyer looking to add an investment property to their portfolio and who is concerned about the timing of the sale, the costs of owning the property, and the ability to rent to tenants in the future. Personal circumstances, such as a new job in the area or an impending divorce, can shape the strategy for a negotiation. Once we have completed our research on the house, the market, and the buyers, we can prepare our tactics for the actual negotiation process.

Our process starts by establishing an anchor—a cognitive bias in which a party in a negotiation tends to give too much weight to the first number put forth in a discussion and then inadequately adjusts from that starting point. This bias is well known in economics and business. Even the Harvard Law School's negotiation program notes that we tend to "fixate on anchors [even though] we know they are irrelevant to the discussion at hand."[5] Anchors are commonly used in retail to bias customer price expectations upward. A classic anchoring example is in apparel. Price tags are labeled with a higher price and then marked down. If we see a jacket that is normally marked at $170, we'll believe the jacket is a really good deal on sale at $99. For most buyers, it is hard not to think that this jacket is selling for almost 40 percent less than it should be priced. Even though there is not another jacket selling for $170, buyers believe they have made a good find and will happily hand over $99. But the jacket itself only cost a few dollars to manufacture, and a similar jacket could be purchased somewhere else for $50.

In real estate, this bias is highly effective, and fortunately, you have an advantage as the seller here. You can anchor the buyer with your list price. This anchor persists through the negotiations. It is hard for someone to negotiate far from the anchor price without providing a compelling case for that shift. Even real estate agents, experts in their field, are famously known for being influenced by the anchoring effect of an initial list price. Mentally, it is much easier for an agent to simply adjust off of an existing price anchor than create a completely independent value estimate.[6]

Here's another way to look at anchoring prices. Take, for example, a listing for an upscale colonial-style home with a pool in the backyard. This house was originally listed for $780,000 but, after sitting on the market for several months, had been priced down to $670,000. Is this house a good deal? For those who are comparing to the original price, yes, it's a great deal at $110,000 below the listing price. For others who understand the local market, the more realistic value is actually in the $650,000 range. The sellers misjudged the value of their property in their market, and the house is still overpriced by $20,000. It is still not a great financial purchase for the buyer looking for a good deal on a property. For sellers, reducing the price of an overpriced home is difficult because of the loss aversion they experience over the potential gains that are no longer going to be realized. However, by reframing the situation and anchoring on the idea that the house is now worth $650,000, selling for $670,000 could be a positive experience.

Once this anchor is established, we continue to prepare for the negotiation by understanding the mind-set of both buyer and seller. Real estate negotiations are complicated, because a house is not just another thing people buy. A house is more than just a structure in which to reside but is an extension of their persona and a physical representation of all that the word *home* means. A home influences their daily life: making meals in the kitchen for their family, spending time in the yard with friends, and commuting daily to work, school, and elsewhere in the community. This personal connection can be a double-edged sword as emotions become involved for both the seller and the buyer.

In your preparation for negotiations, the key is to realize—as well as possible—that potential buyers do not have any sentimental connection to your home and have done only minimal evaluation of it at the time of the offer. The set of child handprints in the concrete slab of the rear patio are not a reminder of innocent childhood but, rather, are seen as a flaw in the smooth concrete and a reminder that someone else lived in the house. As we stated at the outset of this book, the house for sale is no longer a home but a product to be sold. Only rarely will a buyer value a previous owner's personalized items on a property; more often, these will hurt the value.

Emotions on the buyer's side do play an important role though—the buyer is making a life-altering decision in an unfamiliar process. Buyers barely know the property and generally assume the worst. They assume the price is probably too high, they assume deferred maintenance will cause a major system to need repairs shortly after closing, and they assume there is an issue with the neighbor's fence on the property line and a constantly barking dog next door that just so happens to be sleeping during their visit to the house. They also realize they are considering purchasing the most expensive item of their lives with only basic knowledge of what they are purchasing and without knowing exactly how the purchase process works. Buyers are nervous and skeptical and want to protect themselves from future losses.

Buyers and sellers are also in two different places from a financial perspective. Sellers are usually looking to maximize their selling price. They know that selling for a few thousand dollars more will help to pay the "already too high" real estate agent commission and could even help buy the new big-screen TV to go with their own new house purchase. Buyers are less concerned about the specific selling price; rather, they look at the purchase from a cash flow perspective. They are looking at how the price influences their monthly payments and whether they can afford their mortgage payment each month. Buyers are also looking at the cash they have on hand and figuring out the size of their down payment and how to pay for initial renovations to the house.

The buyers and sellers also usually have an agent representing their interests. The agents add to the complexity of communicating back and forth and add their own personalities and emotions into the negotiation process. Furthermore, other third parties, such as mortgage companies, lawyers, home inspectors, surveyors, and contractors, play a role in the process of selling and buying a home. Each of these professionals can potentially complicate the process with performance delays, with unfavorable findings, or even by identifying aspects of the property that kill the potential deal.

THE OPTIONS LANDSCAPE

Developing the landscape of options is an important part of negotiation preparations. We know price is not the sole determinate for a buyer's offer. Several other factors can influence which offer is accepted, including the timing of the offer, the form of financing and expected down payment, the levels of due diligence or earnest monies (use of these terms varies by state), a conditional sale requirement, other requests such as including items to convey or required repairs, and finally, the personal relationships, good or bad, any of the parties have with one another. As part of negotiation preparations, time is well spent to understand the potential terms presented in an offer. Each term has implications, and you should be able to quickly understand each term to judge the overall value of the offer and to respond with a planned and prepared response.

Offer timing

A "normal" residential real estate transaction can take four to eight weeks, depending on the state requirements and mortgage company processes. For sellers, speed to close is an important consideration. Every day that a property is under contract but not yet closed is another day that either a better offer could come along or the deal could fall through. A longer contract time means more time for the buyer to find additional items for repair in the house or for the buyer's financing to fall through. The buyer could have a medical emergency or lose their job. A longer length of time to a closing simply adds risk and uncertainty to the transaction. An offer with a shorter time to close is lower risk and more valuable to both parties, but especially to you as a seller.

Occasionally, though, you might benefit from an extended timeline to close. For buyers looking to relocate out of state or move at the end of a school year, a two- or three-month timeline to close may be in your best interest. In one transaction, my company represented buyers working with an investor flipping a property. The property had been purchased by the seller about 10 months earlier, and at the seller's request, we scheduled the closing to be two months out rather than the buyers' initial preference of one month. Extending the timing would allow the seller to tax their gains differently, giving them an additional financial benefit. This timing did not alter the buyers' plans for the property and allowed the buyers to negotiate a lower price.

Financing

In the United States, government support for homeownership has created a vast array of financial options to purchase a home. Every financing option has its own set of requirements, and you should understand the implications related to the financing program your buyer will use.

The most straightforward form of financing is a cash payment. Here, the buyer simply transfers funds from their account to the seller's in exchange for the property. Although a cash purchase is the least risky form of financing for a seller, you should insist on seeing proof of funds prior to signing a sales contract and should understand that available funds at the time of purchase do not positively guarantee that they will be available by the time of close.

Conventional bank loans are the next most straightforward form of financing. Today's lending institutions tend to be stricter about approving loans than they were in the past but remain a common source of funds. A mortgage company typically requires an appraisal of the home and title insurance to cover its loan.

Government loan programs offer benefits to home buyers with either low down payment requirements or lower interest rates. For you as the seller, these loan programs can have specific conditions that can add some complexity to the closing process. One example of a government program is a US Department of Veterans Affairs (VA) loan. Buyers applying for a VA loan are required to have the house they are purchasing inspected by a VA-approved home inspector. This inspector looks to ensure the house is safe, sound, and sanitary to protect both the veteran buying the property and the financial firm making the loan guaranteed by the federal government. Any major defects found during this inspection process must be corrected prior to the loan approval. This additional required inspection process can lengthen the time to closing compared with other financing alternatives.

The Federal Housing Administration (FHA) is another agency that works with financial firms to help buyers purchase a home. FHA loans usually have low down payments, allowing home buyers with limited savings to purchase a home. One nuance of the FHA process is the appraisal. A home appraisal for the purposes of an FHA loan "sticks" with the home for up to four months. For you, this becomes an issue in a scenario where the appraisal comes in low relative to the contracted price for a buyer, and if you and the buyer cannot agree to bridge the difference, the deal falls apart. If another buyer decides to purchase your home within four months and this buyer is also planning to use an FHA loan, the first low appraisal would still be in effect, requiring either you to lower your price or the buyer to increase their down payment; otherwise, this deal would collapse like the first.

Other less common forms of financing, such as loan assumption or seller financing, can have their uses but remain rare. Each form of proposed financing has implications, and you should understand the differences and how they could impact the sale of your home.

Due diligence and earnest monies

Each state has its own customs and norms for an initial good-faith or earnest money payment to allow the buyer to conduct detailed due diligence on the home. A larger, nonrefundable due diligence amount generally strengthens an offer and provides you with a level of compensation should the transaction not close. A low amount of up-front money could indicate a low level of commitment to purchasing the property or a lack of funds readily available for the purchase, either of which adds uncertainty to the buyer being able to close the sale.

Conditional sale clause

Given the high cost of homeownership, many buyers cannot afford to own two homes at the same time. Furthermore, some buyers commonly have equity for a down payment tied up in the value of an existing home. These buyers need to sell their current home in order to afford their future home, and timing both a house purchase and a sale along with moving between closing is a tricky proposition in the best of conditions. One common contract feature is including the sale of their existing house as a condition for the purchase of the new house. For you, accepting a contract with this language adds significant uncertainty to the transaction and depends on the actions of the buyer, the agent selling the buyer's house, and the specifics of the house and market the house is selling in. If you receive an offer to purchase with a conditional sale clause, understand where and how the house is being sold and propose less risky alternatives, such as a longer timeline to close rather than accepting the buyer's risk of selling their home.

Other requests

In the wild world of residential real estate, the "other" category is a Pandora's box full of stipulations and requirements. Any additional buyer's requests should be considered carefully. Buyers asking for contributions to closing costs or adding a home warranty are easily understood and quantified for consideration in an overall offer. More difficult, however, are the emotional requests. Buyers asking to include Grandpa's stone bench in the backyard, to include the heirloom chandelier that "makes" the dining room, or to remove the old basketball hoop in the driveway can all add friction to a transaction. An outside observer would be astonished at the number of issues related to which appliances stay or go in a transaction.

One method to minimize the risk of a transaction going awry over something small is to associate a dollar figure with each element in question and then compare the dollar amount to the price of the overall transaction. Agreeing to have the 2,500-pound gun safe removed from the basement of a house would make sense in a contract, because that could cost the buyer several thousand dollars if doorframes need to be removed, floors replaced, and so on. The buyer asking for the old freezer in the garage, which could be purchased new for a couple hundred dollars, probably makes less sense to argue about, especially if you otherwise stand to make a healthy profit with the buyer's offer. Most of the "other" items that can cause a heated argument in negotiation represent a financially negligible portion of the overall transaction. Because these emotion-based items can cause a deal to collapse or otherwise create hard feelings for the buyer, seller, and agents involved in the transaction, maintaining an objective mind-set is the best approach to minimize issues with any "other" requests and leads to a straightfor-ward, well-documented, and clean deal.

Personal relationships

Finally, understanding the people in the negotiation can factor into the attractiveness of an offer. A clean deal between two parties that know each other should be expected to be quick and easy. Relationships and reputations between real estate agents factor into these dynam-ics, too. Take the example of a seller who has received two equivalent offers. One is presented by an agent known for their difficult, win-at-all-costs attitude, and the second is presented by an agent who is informed and professional, and the seller's agent has worked with them previously. Here, the seller's agent may recommend that the seller choose the second offer and the expected smoother path to closing. Personalities do matter in the residential real estate space.

Together, the factors of price, timing, financing, conditions, and personalities outline the game board of options for both parties nego-tiating for an accepted offer. You should understand what your ideal offer looks like given the range of options. Good agents also know how to use this information to your advantage and how to shape a deal where both parties win.

CONDUCTING THE NEGOTIATION

Negotiations should begin after the research and preparation have been completed. Negotiations are conducted in one of two ways. The first is an advocate's approach, where the outcome leads to one party winning and the other losing. A second approach is interest-based bargaining, where both parties can have winning outcomes in a transaction. Both approaches have their time and place, but for residential real estate transactions, an interest-based or win-win approach is the best to complete the deal, while also creating optimal outcomes for both you and your buyer.

From a tactical perspective, every back-and-forth in a negotiation consumes time and emotion from both negotiating parties, as well as their agents. There is a cost to creating an offer, communicating the offer, and editing the offer for agreement. For effectiveness, a guiding rule is no more than three rounds of negotiation to get to a deal. If it takes more than three rounds, the gap is probably too big between you and the buyer, or the details have become less and less important. For both you and the buyer, aiming to be complete in three or even two rounds tends to be beneficial, as both parties continue to have a positive feeling about the transaction and do not feel as though they have been taken advantage of to the last remaining bit of value.

Reciprocity is a negotiation best practice and should be considered in your home sale negotiations. As the buyer asks for something, you should ask as well. You should never make a unilateral concession to a buyer—or them to you. From a mental perspective, the party giving can begin to feel pressured and like they are losing, which could cause the deal to fall apart altogether. On the flip side, giving something small in return for a larger take allows both parties to feel like they are winning in the negotiation, even if the value is clearly one-sided.

Another often-provided guideline for negotiations is to never change your reservation price at the negotiation table. A reservation price represents the least favorable but acceptable terms to complete the deal. For sellers, this is usually the lowest price and most unfavorable terms. The research and preparation you completed for the negotiation should provide the confidence and support to insist for offer terms appropriate for the property. Receiving an offer for a house is exciting: Someone wants to give you lots of money for your house! The reality is that you must accept offers that meet your minimum requirements. You should not give away the value in the home to a low-ball offer just because of the excitement and flattery of receiving an offer. Only consider offers meeting your predetermined reservation price, and then enjoy selling your house at a price you will not later regret.

One final bit of advice: Set your internal anchor on your reservation price, not the listing price. The listing price is set to anchor the buyers at the higher price. As a seller, know your minimum reservation price and feel good about settling for a deal over that price. Sellers anchoring their reservation price at the list price are setting themselves up for hard feelings and missed expectations; the list price is just a starting point. Homes that sell above list are the exception and not the rule for residential real estate sales.

Negotiations are a two-way street, but you should be looking to sell for the full value of your home. Your house is the only one like it on the market. If it is properly prepared for sale, properly priced, and properly marketed, it is highly likely that the house will be quickly matched with a ready, willing, and able buyer excited to purchase your home. You have something buyers want and should not be afraid to design a deal that works for you.

FROM CONTRACT TO CLOSE

In residential real estate, the signing of an offer to purchase is not the end of the home-selling process. A contract signing kicks off more detailed due diligence activities for the buyer and requires cooperation from you. Your goal during this phase is to help get the buyer to the closing table as fast as possible while giving up as little value as possible.

After the contract is signed, a prudent buyer begins their due diligence of the property and arranges their financing. Typically, this would mean having the home inspected, the lot surveyed, the title examined, and the property appraised if it is being financed. The buyer will lead these efforts, because it is in their best interest. As a seller, your role is to cooperate with them to allow this due diligence to take place.

The best outcome is one of no surprises. As a seller, if you had the home inspected prior to the listing, pulled a copy of a previous survey, priced the home properly, and kept the title clean, the due diligence should be relatively straightforward. Issues with any of these areas create complications as they reveal challenges with the property that may reduce the price the buyer wishes to pay. Any number of issues can come up during due diligence, but common issues relate to the building structure, the title and related property covenants, and government-related items such as zoning, permits, and services.

At this point in the process, the buyer has invested time and money into the purchase. Any additional investment in due diligence is money they may not get back should they back out of the contract. Each additional cost incurred further invests the buyer in your property, and it will take a major finding for them to exit the contract (but this happens). The buyer's actions during due diligence are mostly out of your control.

During the contract-to-close period, you will typically face two major risks, which you *can* influence: buyer-requested repairs and a delay of closing. Here, you must consider the trade-off of risk versus value to get to the final closing. A home inspection reveals flaws in the home's construction. These can range from minor items like a burned-out light bulb on the porch and a worn roof shingle to major items such as cracks in the foundation or rotted wood components. Depending on the extent of the inspection report's findings, the buyer may ask for some repairs or other financial allowances, or credits, before agreeing to purchase the home. This process varies by state and local custom but is a chance for the buyer to pressure you into concessions in order to close the deal. This threat usually leads to another round of negotiation.

Here, the negotiation process should be similar to negotiating the offer. You should have a good sense of what the buyer's inspection might reveal and should know the related costs to fix the issues. You should understand what options are available to fix the potential issues, such as do the repair yourself, hire a professional, or offer a dollar credit to the buyer at close. If there is a credit, you should have a range and maximum credit in mind and reasoning for it. The idea of a walkaway price is valid here. If a buyer insists on $15,000 of credit for items you believe to already be incorporated into the price of the home, say no. The buyer will then have to decide whether it is worth pulling out of the deal or accepting a lower credit at a number within your reservation price.

In most cases, a credit is the lowest-risk option for repairs beyond changing out a light bulb. The buyer will expect professional quality work with any repairs, and there is the risk that a repair may not actually fix the problem or may create more repairs (such as when the contractor working in the attic steps through the drywall of the ceiling below). Providing your buyer with a credit to resolve reasonable requests is a clean and efficient method to move past any repair requests.

Finally, we know a delayed closing increases your holding costs. Worse, a delayed closing indicates that something is not going according to the original plan when the contract was signed. Many things cause closing delays, such as issues with financing or a hurricane passing through the region. Most of the time, these factors are out of your control, but a proactive approach can be helpful. As the closing date approaches, frequent interactions between you and the buyer or their agent can be helpful, simply to check in. This communication increases transparency in the process, adds a sense of urgency to the closing date, and provides an opportunity for you to assist the process whenever possible, such as adding a signature to an updated form.

The period from contract to close is the last step on the path to selling your home for maximum profit. A well-prepared seller and a vetted buyer should experience few surprises in this last phase, and both sides should expect a smooth closing and successful sale.

CONCLUSION

FOR FULL VALUE

We have covered a lot of content in this book. We started by discussing how "squishy" home prices are and how the uniqueness of each house makes precise pricing impossible. We looked at which factors influence the price of the home, starting at the basic level of supply and demand, including a number of different supply and demand factors and how these combine to affect house prices at a regional or city level. We drilled down to look at what can add value to a house at both the neighborhood level and at the individual home level. We walked through what steps a typical buyer takes on the path toward an offer and how a seller can help the right ready, willing, and able buyer see that the seller's house is the best one for them.

We covered how to prepare a home for sale and what really makes a difference to a buyer. The old real estate agent standbys of clean, declutter, and curb appeal remain important factors in selling a house at the best price possible. We walked through elements of a powerful listing, including professional photography and a well-written description. We also discussed trade-offs between the different pricing strategies and the importance of hiring a professional real estate agent. We provided specific recommendations and the data-backed rationale for each one and discussed why some other actions are not recommended.

Ten specific actions are listed below to help you effectively implement the recommendations outlined in this book. These actions summarize and simplify everything we have covered, with the intent of enabling you to sell your home for a price higher than what would normally be expected. As a seller, you have to be honest in the product you are offering to the market and know that dated houses may not be as attractive to buyers as newly constructed or renovated homes. That reality will help you price your home appropriately to compete with similar homes.

Here are my 10 simple actions you can take to sell your home for full value:

1. Clean the exterior completely.

2. Clean the interior completely.

3. Repaint the kitchen, bathrooms, and master bedroom.

4. Hire a *good, professional* real estate agent.

5. Complete the required property disclosures.

6. Identify all valuable attributes.

7. Use an optimal pricing strategy.

8. Write a detailed listing using key words.

9. Use professional photos in the listing.

10. List at the optimal time of the week and year.

Before we close, I must provide a caveat for my statements by noting that each sale is unique. Every house is different, every buyer is different, and the market and competition continuously change and evolve. What works for some people may not work for others. I cannot guarantee a higher price for everyone; however, I do passionately believe this advice heavily tips the scales in your favor for realizing a higher price or completing a quicker transaction. My goal is to help you realize a 5 percent to 10 percent higher selling price than you would have without taking any other actions.

Good luck!

ACKNOWLEDGMENTS

Creating a book for publication is a more involved endeavor than I ever imagined at the start of this project. For authors, having the support of a team is a necessity, and I would like to thank those who made this book possible.

First, I would like to thank the many real estate experts who answered my questions and helped shape the content, with special thanks to Theresa Lobdell and Matt Demson for their specific feedback and anecdotes.

I would also like to thank the entire team at Allen Tate's Chapel Hill/ Durham office for guiding me as I sought to apply the book's insights in a practical, real-world setting. I would especially like to thank Sandra Paul for her patience and encouragement to explore this topic.

This book would not exist without the dedicated support of the publishing team at Greenleaf Book Group. Tyler LeBleu, Lindsey Clark, Nathan True, Judy Marchman, and Jeffrey Curry were critical to shaping and forming the book into the final product. Neil Gonzalez did an amazing job with the book's graphics and layout.

I would like to give a big thanks to my family for their encouragement and feedback. To Mom and Dad for their opinions and suggestions from start to finish, to Barbara and Dale for their industry perspectives and feedback, and to my brothers, Peter and Andrew, for their comments.

And finally, to my wife, Kristen, this book is the tangible output of many months of hard work that would not have been possible without your full support from idea to finished product. Your insights and contributions helped improve this book tremendously. Thank you!

DOING YOUR OWN
DUE DILIGENCE—
A HOME SELLER
SELF-ASSESSMENT

The following questions serve as a guide to help home sellers think more critically about the process of selling their home and work to optimize the specific action items provided throughout this book and, in particular, the action list included in the conclusion.

The questions are organized by chapter, and I recommend that you work through them as you complete each chapter. The goal is to help you start looking beyond the usual timeworn advice when it comes to selling homes and instead embrace how data can be used to help you get full value for your home.

CHAPTER 1: HOW HOME VALUE IS DETERMINED

The first step to selling your home for full value is to establish a solid baseline or expected selling price—or, more accurately, a zone of pricing uncertainty or a selling pricing range. You want to arrive at an expected selling price that is not outside of that zone—too low and you miss out on revenue, too high and your house could just sit on the market.

To determine your expected selling price, review the following:

- What are the closest comparables or comps to my home that have sold recently or are currently on the market?
- What do automated valuation models (AVMs), such as those used by Zillow, Redfin, or Eppraisal, have my home currently valued at?

Activity:

Like the example shown in this chapter, combine estimates from both your real estate agent and AVMs to create a price range for your home. List three to four comps and three to four AVMs to develop your price range and then take an average to establish an estimated expected selling price.

CHAPTER 2: FACTORS THAT AFFECT HOME VALUE

Two key factors can influence your home's value: its physical location and the improvements you've put into it. Generally speaking, the land your home is on adds value or appreciates over time, while home improvements depreciate due to the money and time that go into maintaining your home. This chapter focuses on your home's location and how it can affect the home's value.

Think about your home's location from three perspectives: regional, neighborhood, and actual home/lot. How do each of these perspectives affect your home's value? Delve deep into each level with the following questions.

At the regional level:

- What is the population growth in your area?
- What are your region's demographics?
- How is the local economy doing and what kind of jobs or industry is in the area?
- What are the physical attributes of your region?

At the neighborhood level:

- What is the age of your neighborhood—what's the average age of the houses?
- Is there an HOA?
- Proximity to jobs—what's the commute time?
- Access to public transportation or area highways?
- What is your neighborhood's walkability?

- Proximity to area amenities such as shopping, dining, or social activities?

- What are the school ratings for the district your home is zoned for?

- What have homes in your neighborhood or surrounding neighborhoods sold for recently?

- How has your neighborhood changed since you've lived there?

At the house/lot level:

- What is the size of your home's lot and its geographic orientation?

- Is the lot on a cul-de-sac or corner?

- What is your home's livable square footage?

- What style of home do you have, and does it resonate with current buyers?

Activity:

Discuss your answers with your real estate agent to determine how your home's location could affect your home's value for better or worse. Going forward, we'll look at factors you can use to accentuate your home's positive features and mitigate any negative ones.

Dive Deeper:

Do you know how your home is being valued by appraisers? This is helpful information, particularly going into a contract when an appraiser is brought in to validate the home's sales price.

CHAPTER 3: FINDING VALUE

Old-school wisdom for increasing the value of your home usually refers to making some sort of update or renovation. However, when you invest in a home renovation (new floors, new kitchen or bath) for the sole purpose of getting more money when you sell, you may be disappointed with the actual financial return.

First ask yourself:

- Will the potential payback on the investment justify making the improvement?
- Do I understand this difference between the cost of the project and the total value it will add to my home (reflected in the potential selling price)?

Then ask:

- Where can I highlight value in my home without making a major change?
- What are the differentiators and bonuses that make my home unique to buyers?
- Does your home have any "green" or environmentally friendly features such as solar panels?
- What about trees in your yard (front and back) or green spaces and walking/biking paths throughout your neighborhood?

Activity:

List your differentiators and bonuses and discuss potential value with your real estate agent.

CHAPTER 4: FIRST IMPRESSIONS: CURB APPEAL

In preparing your home for sale, the data support the value of curb appeal when it comes to positively affecting a home's selling price.

Your home's exterior:

- How does your home's curb appeal stack up to your neighbors' homes or other homes in the neighborhood?

- What features on your home's exterior stand out, good *and* bad?

- Are there any obvious problems or items that need cleaning, repairing, or replacing?

- Does your home look dated or modern and appealing? Is the front door (and door knob) in good condition?

Your home's landscaping:

- Do you have a well-kept lawn or other landscaping features such as hardscapes that are in good shape?

- What about trees and bushes or other plants?

- Are your driveway and sidewalks in good shape?

- Will your landscaping need more serious improvements, such as laying new sod or fixing a fence, or are there simple things you can do, such as added some flowering plants or trimming bushes?

Activity:

Create a to-do list for sprucing up your home's exterior and landscaping. Separate and prioritize major updates (new sod or a new exterior paint job) and minor, quick fixes (adding potted plants, trimming up bushes) based on your budget and selling timeframe.

CHAPTER 5: I COULD LIVE HERE

Once you've got your exterior projects lined up, it's time to tackle the interior. This chapter looks at depersonalizing, decluttering, and staging your home.

Decluttering goes hand in hand with depersonalizing. You'll likely do both at the same time. A decluttered house presents a calmer, more soothing experience for potential buyers.

What does a good depersonalized and decluttered home look like? Think of those beautifully staged yet impersonal homes seen in the media. You want buyers to be able to envision themselves in the home instead of trying to look past all of your stuff.

While you don't necessarily need to repaint everything in neutrals, consider which colors might be off-putting to buyers. Consider creating pops of color on feature walls.

To depersonalize and declutter:

- What items would you need to remove from view? Family photos? Unique artwork? Shelves full of collectibles and trinkets?
- Do you have unique or personal paint colors throughout the home?
- Beyond your personal items, what other things can you clean out?
- Can you see your kitchen table? Or your kitchen counters?

- Is your garage packed so full you can't park in it?

- Can you see the back of your master closet?

- Do you have piles of stuff lying around, like old magazines or your children's old school papers or toys?

To deep clean your home:

- If you have carpet, does it need to be steam cleaned?

- What about cleaning your window treatments (blinds, curtains)?

- What about the bathrooms and the kitchen?

To stage your home for sale:

- Should you hire someone to stage your home?

- Or are there things you can do yourself to effectively stage your home after depersonalizing, decluttering, and cleaning?

- Evaluate the cost of staging versus the potential benefit of selling your home faster and for more.

- Discuss with your real estate agent whether staging would be beneficial for your particular home and market.

Activity:

Think about how you could stage your home to present it in its best light without too much additional cost. Consider other steps and costs involved, such as starting to pack up your home and renting a storage facility for your things.

CHAPTER 6: THE BUYER'S PERSPECTIVE

What actions can you take to ensure that buyers who are looking for a property like yours can find it? And then, how do you get them interested in buying your home? In other words, how do you market your home?

This chapter looks at the process buyers goes through to purchase a home: the buyer funnel. We look at the following stages:

- Research
- Shortlist
- Comparison
- Visiting Properties
- Making an Offer
- Closing the Deal

Ask yourself:

- What differentiators and bonuses can you highlight at each stage of the buyer funnel to keep buyers interested?
- Of particular importance is the comparison stage: What features make your home stand out to comparables?
- How can you reduce buyer risk?
- What potential concerns might buyers have about your home, and what information can you provide to ease their minds?
- Are all mandated property disclosures completed and available?
- What additional information can you provide to help buyers get to know your home (e.g., copy of deed, recent home inspection, a survey, warranties, recent HOA meeting minutes)?

- Do you have a home warranty that covers key systems, such as HVAC?

Activity:

By the time you meet the buyer, they should be at the end stages of the buyer funnel. Consider your home from the buyer's perspective at each stage. What information would you look for about your home, and what questions would you want to know the answers to? Looking back at the lessons of Chapter 5, would a buyer be able to see themself living there? (Be honest!)

CHAPTER 7: SETTING THE LIST PRICE

Arriving at a listing price is challenging because of the many factors that go into it. So how do you find that just right price? In this chapter we discuss three pricing strategies:

- *Round number strategy*—Indicates that a seller is easy to work with and willing to negotiate, but could also signal seller uncertainty to the buyer.
- *Just below strategy*—Indicates the seller is willing to negotiate but with the intent to negotiate down to the target sales price.
- *Precise strategy*—Indicates a seller who is very detailed and has done their homework in developing the listing price. But this could also signal that the seller will not be as willing to negotiate or be nitpicky about every item.

Deciding which strategy to use depends on your desired outcome for your sales price. How do you define your desired outcome for your home's sale price?

Do you need to make a certain amount or a certain percentage over listing price? Or are you ok if you sell at list price?

Activity:

Take your selling price range and estimated expected selling price from Chapter 1 and apply each of the three pricing strategies to it. Which strategy appeals to you or are you most comfortable with using? Discuss this with your real estate agent as well to get their input on the different pricing strategies.

CHAPTER 8: DEVELOPING AN EFFECTIVE LISTING

Having a well-thought-out and thorough home listing can keep interested buyers moving through your buyer funnel and help land your home on their shortlists. This chapter examines the various factors that go into developing that listing, starting with your home's photos—because a good exterior photo is the first thing buyers are going to look for.

You'll want bright, clear professional images. How will your real estate agent arrange for home photography for your listing?

Where does your home rank based on quality of materials and

features: high-end, mid-tier, or low-tier? And how do your home's features compare to those of other homes in your neighborhood?

To ensure your home is comparable to the next aspirational level, how do you help your real estate agent identify your home's differentiators and bonus features to highlight in your listing?

In drafting your listing description, has your agent used words that signal a small size, advanced age, or low quality? Which words can potentially elevate sales price—and which ones could you use for your listing?

Activity:

While your agent will write the official listing, try writing your own listing description using the tips in Chapter 8 and then compare and discuss it with your agent to put together a strong final description.

CHAPTER 9: TIMING: WHEN TO MARKET

This chapter looks at how crucial timing is when it comes to listing your home.

From a seasonal standpoint, do you need to sell your home right away (such as for a job transfer)? Or can you be more selective in what time of year you list your home?

For your geographic region, what are the optimal times of year to list?

Once you decide what time of year to list, of equal importance is what day of the week. As we learned, listing your home close to or on the weekend can draw greater buyer interest because that's when they are typically going to be out looking.

That leads us to the next step:

- How can you maximize that buyer interest during the crucial first 14-day window your home is on the market?

- Do you have an open house scheduled for the first weekend after listing?

Activity:

Discuss marketing and promotional efforts with your real estate agent and establish an action plan for the first 14 days after listing.

CHAPTER 10: SELECTING A GOOD AGENT

Selecting a real estate agent is like selecting any contractor: They have to know what they're doing and also be a good fit for you and your goals for selling your home. Here are two key questions to ask potential real estate agents to ensure you get a true professional:

- How many transactions have you done in the last 12 months?

- What value do you provide me relative to other agents? (Value considerations: home valuation, listing, marketing, and negotiation)

Activity:

Get several recommendations for real estate agents and put together a list to compare them, including their experience, credentials, knowledge of homes in your area—and most important, their answers to the above questions.

CHAPTER 11: NEGOTIATION

In this chapter, we discuss the three main phases of negotiation: research, planning, and completing the deal. Your real estate agent can handle the actual communications but they have to know your negotiating numbers to be truly effective. Before actual negotiations start, you should have a well-defined point below which you will be willing to walk away: your reservation price (your internal anchor).

- What does your ideal offer look like given the range of options available to you and the buyer during negotiation (price, timing, financing, conditions, personalities)?

- What kind of research can you undertake on the buyer to determine what the buyer views as a good deal?

- What does your local residential real estate market look like: is it a buyer's or a seller's market?

- How can these market factors affect how buyers see your home and the price it should bring?

- Is the market more in your favor as a seller or the buyer's? If the latter, how can you adjust your negotiation expectations and tactics to create a positive outcome?

- Your buyer's anchor is your list price. How does that anchor affect how buyers will negotiate the sales price?

- Using the negotiation method of interest-based bargaining— both parties have the best opportunity to achieve a winning outcome—what does that winning outcome look like to you?

- If you're asked to make a concession, what concession do you ask the buyer in return? Or is there a smaller concession you can make to ensure a successful transaction?

Activity:

Think about setting your reservation price—this is the price you have to feel good with getting, if it comes to that. Discuss negotiation strategies with your real estate agent to ensure you get the amount for your home that is ultimately satisfactory to you.

CHAPTER 12: FROM CONTRACT TO CLOSE

Once the house is under contract, you are largely in a wait-and-see period as the buyer conducts their due diligence, such as an inspection. But there are two keys areas where you can influence the situation: buyer-requested repairs and a delay of closing.

What are the trade-offs of risk vs. value to ensure you reach closing?

Consider your options for dealing with buyer-requested repairs that stay within your reservation price. Are you prepared to walk away from the deal if necessary?

How can you stay proactive in interacting with the buyer during a closing delay?

Activity:

Outline potential asks from the buyer during the closing period along with the related costs and options to fix those issues. For example, if you know that your home needs a new roof, it might be more cost-effective and less risky for you to offer dollar credits to the buyer so they can complete the repair to their satisfaction.

NOTES

PREFACE

1. Remodeling. 2019. "2018 Cost vs. Value Report." Accessed July 25, 2019. https://www.remodeling.hw.net/cost-vs-value/2018.

2. The calculations are as follows: $392,000 home price times 5 percent sales price increase times 6 percent commission times 50 percent agent split times 80 percent broker split.

INTRODUCTION

1. Kopf, Dan. 2017. "Data analytics have made the NBA unrecognizable." Quartz. October 18, 2017. Accessed February 6, 2019. https://qz.com/1104922/data-analytics-have-revolutionzied-the-nba.

2. Atkins, Charles, Maria Valdivieso De Uster, Mitra Mahdavian, and Lareina Yee. 2016. "Unlocking the Power of Data in Sales." McKinsey & Company, December 2016. https://www.mckinsey.com/business-functions/marketing-and-sales/our-insights/unlocking-the-power-of-data-in-sales.

3. US Bureau of the Census 2018. "Real Median Household Income in the United States" [MEHOINUSA672N]. April 15, 2018. Retrieved from FRED, Federal Reserve Bank of St. Louis. https://fred.stlouisfed.org/series/MEHOINUSA672N.

4. US Bureau of the Census 2018.

5. National Association of Realtors. 2018. "Quick Real Estate Statistics." May 11, 2018. https://www.nar.realtor/research-and-statistics/quick-real-estate-statistics.

6. Adomatis, Sandra. 2018. "Green Homes Sales Prices in Northern California." January 2018. https://www.builditgreen.org/images/BIG_Green_Home_Sales_Prices_Report_FINAL_2018.pdf.

CHAPTER 1

1. www.iaao.org/media/Exposure/AVM_Exposure_9-8-2017_1.docx.

2. Kussin, Zachary. 2016. "Real estate CEO ironically overpays for his own $20M home." *New York Post.* July 12, 2016. https://nypost.com/2016/07/12/real-estate-ceo-ironically-overpays-for-his-own-18m-home.

3. Kussin 2016.

4. Zillow. n.d. "Zestimate." Accessed July 22, 2019. https://www.zillow.com/zestimate.

5. Trulia. 2018. "What is a Trulia Estimate?" September 24, 2018. https://www.trulia.com/trulia_estimates.

6. We could discuss this concept with its caveats and applications in much greater detail but will purposely remain at the basic level for the purposes of this writing.

7. Priceonomics. 2014. "Fact Checking the New York Times and Redfin." March 5, 2014. https://priceonomics.com/fact-checking-the-new-york-times-and-redfin.

CHAPTER 2

1. Galaty, Filmore A., Wellington J. Allaway, and Robert C. Kyle. 2017. Modern Real Estate Practice in North Carolina. La Crosse, WI: Dearborn Real Estate Education.

2. Calder, Vanessa Brown. 2017. "Zoning, Land-Use Planning, and Housing Affordability." CATO Institute Policy Analysis. October 18, 2017. Number 823. https://object.cato.org/sites/cato.org/files/pubs/pdf/pa-823.pdf.

3. Galaty, Allaway, and Kyle 2017.

4. *Realtor Magazine.* 2016. "Good Schools Give Boost to Home Values." August 8, 2016. Accessed October 8, 2018. https://magazine.realtor/daily-news/2016/08/08/good-schools-give-77-boost-home-values.

5. Figlio, David N., and Maurice E. Lucas. "What's In a Grade? School Report Cards and the Housing Market." *American Economic Review* 94(June 2004): 591–604. http://www.nber.org/papers/w8019.pdf.

6. Max, Sarah. 2010. "Good Schools, Bad Real Estate." *The Wall Street Journal.* June 25, 2010. Accessed October 8, 2018. https://www.wsj.com/articles/SB10001424052748704009804575308951902854896.

7. Miller, Jonathan. 2016. "The Relationship Between Commute Time and Housing Prices." Matrix Blog. https://www.millersamuel.com/the-relationship-between-commute-time-and-housing-prices.

8. Henly, Sam. 2018. "Seattle Commuting Costs: Sacrificing 15 Minutes Can Save Thousands." Zillow Research. March 21, 2018. https://www.zillow.com/research/seattle-commuting-costs-savings-19069.

9. Henly 2018.

10. Henly 2018.

11. US Department of Housing and Urban Development, Creating Walkable and Bikeable Communities. 40. https://www.huduser.gov/portal/sites/default/files/pdf/Creating-Walkable-Bikeable-Communities.pdf.

12. Walk Score provides a similar analysis for transit and biking.

13. Rascoff, Spencer, and Stan Humphries. 2015. *Zillow Talk: Rewriting the Rules of Real Estate*. New York: Grand Central Publishing.

14. Bokhari, Sheharyar. 2016. "How Much Is a Point of Walk Score Worth?" Redfin Real-Time (blog), August 3, 2016.

15. "Average Size of US Homes, Decade by Decade." Newser. May 29, 2016. https://www.newser.com/story/225645/average-size-of-us-homes-decade-by-decade.html.

16. Keating, Nathaniel. 2014. "The Corner House and Relative Property Values." Duke University Urban Economics (blog), April 8, 2014. https://sites.duke.edu/urbaneconomics/?p=1194.

17. Asabere, Paul K. 1990. "The Value of a Neighborhood Street Reference to a Cul-de-Sac." *The Journal of Real Estate Finance and Economics* 3(2): 185–193.

18. Appraisals are completed for many reasons outside of providing a bank with an opinion of value related to a loan. People order appraisals to establish fair value of a property for tax purposes, for a private sale, and for setting prices for unique properties.

19. Eriksen, Michael D., Hamilton B. Fout, Mark Palim, and Eric Rosenblatt. 2016. "Contract Price Confirmation Bias: Evidence from Repeat Appraisals" (working paper, October 28, Fannie Mae).

20. Eriksen et al. "Contract Price Confirmation Bias."

CHAPTER 3

1. Remodeling 2018.

2. RESNET. 2018. "What is the HERS Index." Accessed October 19, 2018. http://www.hersindex.com/hers-index/what-is-the-hers-index.

3. RESNET 2018.

4. Adomatis, Sandra. 2018. "Green Homes Sales Prices in Northern California." January 2018. https://www.builditgreen.org/images/BIG_Green_Home_Sales_Prices_Report_FINAL_2018.pdf.

5. Adomatis 2018.

6. NCSolarNow. 2019. "Home Appraisers See a Premium for Rooftop Solar." Accessed October 19, 2019. https://ncsolarnow.com/home-appraisers-see-a-premium-for-rooftop-solar.

7. Wolf, K.L. 2010. "Community Economics—A Literature Review." In *Green Cities: Good Health* (www.greenhealth.washington.edu). College of the Environment, University of Washington. https://depts.washington.edu/hhwb/Thm_Economics.html.

8. Dimke, Kelley C., T. Davis Sydnor, and David S. Gardner. 2013. "The Effect of Landscape Trees on Residential Property Values of Six Communities in Cincinnati, Ohio." *Arboriculture & Urban Forestry* 39 (3): 49–55.

9. GreenBlue Urban. 2017. "How Trees Increase Property Values." August 3, 2017. https://www.greenblue.com/na/how-trees-increase-property-values.

10. The opposite is also true. Low-income neighborhoods in many of these same cities have few trees. Large trees require decades to grow to full size, and the impact of decisions made long ago can be felt today. I commend New York City for its recently completed Million Trees program, in which the city planted more than one million new trees in the city limits, including thousands of new street trees. I believe this will be an investment New York will be proud of in the years ahead.

CHAPTER 4

1. Elam, Emmett, and Andrea Stigarll. 2012. "Landscape and House Appearance Impacts on the Price of Single-Family Homes." *Journal of Environmental Horticulture* 30, no. 4 (December): 182–188. http://hrijournal.org/doi/abs/10.24266/0738-2898.30.4.182.

2. Elam and Stigarll 2012.

3. Elam and Stigarll 2012.

4. Niemiera, Alex X. n.d. "The Effect of Landscape Plants on Perceived Home Value." Virginia Cooperative Extension, Publication 426-087.

5. Henry, Mark. 1994. "The Contribution of Landscaping to the Price of Single Family Homes: A Study of Home Sales in Greenville, South Carolina." *Journal of Environmental Horticulture* 12 (2): 65–70.

CHAPTER 5

1. White, Martha. 2017. "Paint Your Bathroom This Color and Your Home Could Be Worth $5,000 More." *Money*, June 2, 2017. Accessed January 16, 2019. http://time.com/money/4800141/paint-color-higher-home-prices.

2. Saxbe, D., and R. L. Repetti. 2010. "No Place Like Home: Home Tours Predict Daily Patterns of Mood and Cortisol." *Personality and Social Psychology Bulletin* 36(1): 71–81. doi:10.1177/0146167209352864.

3. Arnold, J. E., and U. Lang. 2007. "The Changing Landscape of Home: Trends in Home-Based Leisure and Storage among Working American Families." *Journal of Family and Economic Issues* 28(1): 23–48.

4. "35 Surprising Home Garage Stats You Might Not Know." Garage Living (blog). Accessed February 6, 2019. https://www.garageliving.com/blog/home-garage-stats.

5. Saxbe and Repetti 2010.

6. Gambelin, Anne-Marie. n.d. "It's Science: Clutter Can Actually Give You Anxiety." Motherly (blog). https://www.mother.ly/life/its-science-clutter-can-actually-give-you-anxiety.

7. Lane, Mark A., Michael J. Seiler, and Vicky L. Seiler. 2015. "The Impact of Staging Conditions on Residential Real Estate Demand." *Journal of Housing Research* 24 (1): 21–36. http://aresjournals.org/doi/abs/10.5555/1052-7001.24.1.21?code=ares-site.

8. Real Estate Staging Association. 2019. "Home Staging Infographic." Accessed

January 16, 2019. https://www.realestatestagingassociation.com/content.
aspx?page_id=22&club_id=304550&module_id=164548.

CHAPTER 6

1. Wiebe, Jamie. 2015. "By the Numbers: Who's Buying Homes These Days?"
    Realtor.com. October 20, 2015. https://www.realtor.com/advice/buy/
    normal-home-buying-habits-behavior.

2. Each state has its own set of laws regulating the home-buying process. In North
    Carolina, for example, residential home buyers usually have a due diligence period
    during which they can back out of the sales contract for any or no reason at all as long
    as this is communicated to the sellers during the designated period. There is usually,
    but not always, a payment for this right. Other states have different processes and
    norms.

3. Zillow. 2016. "The Zillow Group Report on Consumer Housing
    Trends." October 18, 2016. https://www.zillow.com/research/
    zillow-group-report-2016-13279/#selectpurchase.

4. There are two schools of thought regarding sharing information beyond what is legally
    required by each state. The first, and the one I fall into, is share as much information as
    possible with the caveat that each piece of information has to be correct. The second
    school is to withhold all information beyond what legally needs to be disclosed.
    Lawyers selling their homes are known to do this to limit their potential liability
    should any information happen to be incorrect or misinterpreted. This approach
    is overly cautious and minimizes risk for the seller. While logically sound, I do not
    believe the latter approach is helpful to the overall success of the transaction.

5. Nanda, Anupam. 2006. "Property Condition Disclosure Law: Does 'Seller Tell
    All' Matter in Property Values?" *Economics Working Papers.* 200547. http://
    digitalcommons.uconn.edu/econ_wpapers/200547.

6. Service Contract Industry Council. 2014. "New Study: Home Warranties Increase
    Home Sale Prices, Reduce Length on the Market for Owners." June 9, 2014. https://
    go-scic.com/2014/06/new-study-home-warranties-increase-home-sale-prices-reduce-
    length-on-the-market-for-owners.

CHAPTER 7

1. Bizer, George Y., and Robert M. Schindler. 2005. "Direct Evidence of Ending-Digit
    Drop-Off in Price Information Processing." *Psychology and Marketing* 22 (10):
    771–783.

2. Rogers, Teri Karush. 2007. "The Psychology of Pricing." *The New York Times*, February
    18, 2007. Accessed February 5, 2019. https://www.nytimes.com/2007/2/18/
    realestate/18cov.html.

3. Cardella, Eric, and Michael J. Seiler. 2016. "The Effect of Listing Price Strategy on Real

Estate Negotiations: An Experimental Study," *Framed Field Experiments* 00623, The Field Experiments Website.

4. Beracha, Eli, and Michael J. Seiler. 2014. "The Effect of Listing Price Strategy on Transaction Selling Prices." *The Journal of Real Estate Finance and Economics* 49: 237–255. 10.1007/s11146-013-9424-1.

5. Rascoff, Spencer, and Stan Humphries. 2015. *Zillow Talk: The New Rules of Real Estate*. New York: Grand Central Publishing, 144.

6. Thomas, Manoj, Daniel H. Simon, and Vrinda Kadiyali. 2007. "Do Consumers Perceive Precise Prices to Be Lower than Round Prices? Evidence from Laboratory and Market Data." September 2007. Johnson School at Cornell University Research Paper No. 09-07. Available at SSRN: https://ssrn.com/abstract=1011232. or http://dx.doi.org/10.2139/ssrn.1011232.

CHAPTER 8

1. National Association of Realtors Research Department. 2018. "Home Buyer and Seller Generational Trends Report 2018." March 2018. https://www.nar.realtor/sites/default/files/documents/2018-home-buyers-and-sellers-generational-trends-03-14-2018.pdf.

2. Older buyers still use the internet to find homes, although to a lesser degree than younger buyers. Older home buyers still primarily find the homes they purchase through a real estate agent.

3. Seiler, Michael J., Poornima Madhavan, and Molly Liechty. 2012. "Toward an Understanding of Real Estate Homebuyer Internet Search Behavior: An Application of Ocular Tracking Technology." March 27, 2012. *Journal of Real Estate Research*, 34 (2). Available at SSRN: https://ssrn.com/abstract=2029823.

4. Allison, Melissa. 2015. "4 Ways to Tell How Fast Your Home Will Sell." Zillow Porchlight (blog), July 13, 2015. https://www.zillow.com/blog/tell-how-fast-home-will-sell-178449.

5. Hochberg, Emily. 2019. "Homes Listed with Professional Real Estate Photos Sell Quicker and for More Money." Redfin Real-Time Research (blog), June 3, 2019. https://www.redfin.com/blog/2013/12/professional-photos-2013.html.

6. Rascoff, Spencer, and Stan Humphries. 2015. *Zillow Talk: The New Rules of Real Estate*. New York: Grand Central Publishing, 115.

7. Rascoff and Humphries 2015, 111.

8. Rascoff and Humphries 2015, 113–114.

9. Rascoff and Humphries 2015, 113.

CHAPTER 9

1. Bretz, Lauren. 2018. "Why Late Spring Is the Best Time to List a Home For Sale." Zillow Research (blog), March 29, 2018. https://www.zillow.com/research/best-time-to-list-2018-19215.

2. Anderson, Jamie. 2017. "The Whens of Our Sales: Strategy Tips for Timing the

Housing Market When Selling a Home." Zillow Research (blog), March 2, 2017. https://www.zillow.com/research/best-time-to-list-2017-14336.

3. Sipola, Chris. 2016. "The Price of Overpricing: How Listing Price Impacts Time on Market." Zillow Research (blog), May 24, 2016. https://www.zillow.com/research/overpricing-impacts-time-market-12476.

CHAPTER 10

1. National Association of Realtors. 2019. Research Division Home Buyer and Seller Generational Trends Report 2019. Accessed July 25, 2019. https://www.nar.realtor/sites/default/files/documents/2019-home-buyer-and-seller-generational-trends-04-03-2019.pdf.

2. *The Economist*. 2012. "The Great Realtor Rip-Off." May 5, 2012. Accessed February 3, 2019. https://www.economist.com/business/2012/05/05/the-great-realtor-rip-off.

3. Gautier, Pieter, Arjen Siegmann, and Aico van Vuuren. 2018. "Real Estate Agent Performance and Fee Structure." VOX. February 27, 2018. https://voxeu.org/article/real-estate-agent-performance-and-fee-structure.

4. In many cases, the law requires real estate agents to act in the best interest of their clients, which should apply here, as well. Unfortunately, the distinction between a suboptimal but acceptable outcome and an outcome not in the client's best interest is difficult to determine and even more difficult to prove.

5. Levitt, Steven D., and Chad Syverson. 2008. "Market Distortions When Agents Are Better Informed: The Value of Information in Real Estate Transactions." *The Review of Economics and Statistics*. MIT Press. Vol. 90 (4) (November): 599–611.

6. Bernheim, B. Douglas, and Jonathan Meer. 2013. "Do Real Estate Brokers Add Value When Listing Services Are Unbundled?" *Economic Inquiry* 51: 1166–1182. doi:10.1111/j.1465-7295.2012.00473.x.

7. Jia, Panle, and Parag A. Pathak. 2011. "The Cost of Free Entry: An Empirical Study of Real Estate Agents in Greater Boston." *The RAND Journal of Economics* 46. 10.1111/1756-2171.12082.

8. National Association of Realtors. 2018. "Quick Real Estate Statistics."

9. National Association of Realtors. 2018. "Quick Real Estate Statistics."

CHAPTER 11

1. Subramanian, Guhan. 2019. "What is BATNA? How to Find Your Best Alternative to a Negotiated Agreement." Harvard Law School Program on Negotiation (blog), May 7, 2019. https://www.pon.harvard.edu/daily/batna/translate-your-batna-to-the-current-deal.

2. Kahneman, D., and Tversky, A. 1979. "Prospect Theory: An Analysis of Decision under Risk." *Econometrica* 47 (4): 263–291. CiteSeerX 10.1.1.407.1910. doi:10.2307/1914185. JSTOR 1914185.

3. Allen Tate Realtors. 2018. "The Science of a Changing Market." Presentation, Charlotte, North Carolina.

4. Allen Tate Realtors 2018.

5. Shonk, Katie. 2019. "What Is Anchoring in Negotiation?" Harvard Law School Program on Negotiation (blog). February 19, 2019. https://www.pon.harvard.edu/daily/negotiation-skills-daily/what-is-anchoring-in-negotiation.

6. Anchors can be a powerful tool for agents to use when showing homes to potential buyers. Statements such as "you'll love the amazing kitchen" or "the backyard is incredible" sets the anchor for buyers, who will view the kitchen as "amazing" or the backyard as "incredible." Such is the power of cognitive biases.

INDEX

A

A/B testing, 102–3
adjusted comparables, 15, 18–20
Adomatis, Sandra, 9
advocate's approach, 155
agents, real estate. *See* real estate agents
amateur versus professional photos, 105–7
amenities, proximity to, 33–34
American Home Shield, 88
anchor, establishing, 145–46, 156
appliance warranties and receipts, 87
appraisers, role of, 36–39, 170
appreciation of land, 25–27
ATTOM Data Solutions, 30
attributes of home, highlighting. *See* differ-
        entiators, highlighting
Austin, Texas, green premium in, 46
automated valuation models (AVMs), 92,
        168
    baseline price, establishing, 18–20
    general discussion, 15–18

B

bank loans, 150
baseline price
    establishing, 18–24
    region, impact on, 28–29
bathroom remodels, 41–43

Beracha, Eli, 95–96
best alternative to a negotiated agreement
        (BATNA), 138
best practices, 162–63, ix–xix
bias
    anchor, establishing, 145–46, 156
    of appraisers, 38–39
big-data approach, 9–10
bonus features, highlighting
    during buyer funnel phases, 82–84
    green energy ratings, 44–47
    home seller self-assessment of, 171
    in listing description, 109–14
    solar panels, 47–49
buyer funnel
    closing phase, 82
    comparison phase, 81
    differentiators, highlighting, 82–84
    first 14 days of listing, importance of,
        120
    home seller self-assessment of, 175–76
    keeping in mind, 89
    offer phase, 82
    overview, 79
    research phase, 80
    shortlist phase, 80
    visiting phase, 81
buyer perspective. *See also* buyer funnel
    buyer risk, reducing, 84–89
    differentiators, highlighting, 82–84

overview, 77–78
buyer-requested repairs, 158–59, 181–82
buyer risk, reducing, 84–89
buyer's market, identifying
    with days on market, 142
    general discussion, 140–42
    with list-price-to-close ratio, 143
    with market price appreciation, 144–48
    with months of inventory, 142–43
    with number of showings, 143
    submarkets, 141

C

California, green premium in, 45–46
Cardella, Eric, 95
cash purchases, 150
CATO Institute, 29
Center on Everyday Lives of Families
    (CELF), 67–68
certification, green, 44–47
charm pricing, 93
cleaning
    decluttering, 67–70
    exterior of home, 61
    interior of home, 70, 173–74
climate, effect on property value, 28–29
closing
    buyer funnel phase, 82
    contract-to-close period, 157–60
    delays in, 159–60, 181
    overview, 7
    timing options, 149–50
clutter in homes, cleaning out, 67–70,
    173–74
color of interior paint, choosing, 65–66, 72
commissions, xviii
    iBuyers, 131–32
    for real estate agents, 125, 127, 128–29
commute time, impact on property value,
    31–33
comparables method, 15, 18–20, 92
comparing exterior with others in neigh-
    borhood, 56–57
comparison phase, buyer funnel, 81, 82–83
conditional sale clause, 152
conducting negotiations, 154–56

confirmation bias, 38–39
contract-to-close period
    general discussion, 157–60
    home seller self-assessment for, 181–82
corner lots, value of, 35
cortisol levels, effect of messy homes on,
    68–69
costs
    of buyer-requested repairs, 158–59
    of home renovations, 41–43
    of staging, 71
"Cost vs. Value Report" (*Remodeling* mag-
    azine), 42
cul-de-sac lots, value of, 35–36
curb appeal. *See also* landscaping
    data on, 58–59
    exterior, 56–57
    home seller self-assessment of, 172–74
    increasing, 60–62
    overview, 55–56
    photos in listings, 104–7

D

data
    creating value with, 6–10
    on curb appeal, 58–59
    data analytics, 2–6
    overview, 1–2
    on staging, 70–72
days on market, identifying market trends
    with, 142
day to list, choosing, 119, 179
decluttering, 67–70, 173–74
décor, removing, 64–65
deed, copies of, 84–89
delayed closing, 159–60, 181
demand for homes, 22–23
depersonalizing, 64–65
depreciation of buildings, 25–27
descriptions, writing, 107–14
    differentiators, including, 109–11
    examples of, 112–14
    home seller self-assessment for, 177–78
    length of, 108
    selection of words, 108–9

development policies, effect on property value, 29
differentiators, highlighting, 43–49
  during buyer funnel phases, 82–84
  green energy ratings, 44–47
  home seller self-assessment of, 171
  in listing description, 109–14
  solar panels, 47–49
dirty homes, impact on sales, 70
disclosure forms, 84–89
distribution of potential selling prices, 23–24
driveways, 57–58, 61
due diligence, 82. *See also* home seller self-assessment
  buyer risk, reducing, 84–89
  in contract-to-close period, 157–58
  options related to, 152

E

earnest money payment, 152
economic growth, effect on property value, 29
emotional requests in negotiation, 153
emotions, role in negotiation, 146–47
employment rates, effect on property value, 29
empty versus staged homes, 71
ENERGY STAR certified homes program, 44
EPA (US Environmental Protection Agency) ratings, 44
expected selling price, setting, 18–20
exterior of home
  data on, 58–59
  general discussion, 56–57
  home seller self-assessment of, 172–73
  improving, 60–62

F

faculty staff housing (FSH), Stanford University, 127–28
Fannie Mae, 38–39
Federal Housing Administration (FHA), 151

financing options, 150–51
first impression of house, 55–56
flood risk, 85–86
Florida, study on school quality and property value in, 30–31
14 days following listing, importance of, 120–21, 179
FSH (faculty staff housing), Stanford University, 127–28
funnel, buyer. *See* buyer funnel

G

gains versus losses, psychology of, 138–39
garages, decluttering, 68
gardens, 57–58
Golden Path
  data on, 58–59
  exterior, 56–57
  increasing curb appeal, 60–62
  landscaping, 57–58
  overview, 55–56
good-faith payment, 152
governmental control on real estate agents, 124
government loan programs, 150–51
government policies, effect on property value, 29
granite surfaces, 110–11
grass, 57–58
green energy ratings, 44–47
Green Globes, 44
GreenPoint Rated, 44

H

hedonic regression, 8, 9
HERS (Home Energy Rating System), 44–45, 47
high-end homes, listing descriptions for, 109–11
high precise strategy, 95–98, 99
home décor, removing, 64–65
Home Energy Rating System (HERS), 44–45, 47
home inspections, 84–89, 158
home purchase appraisals, 36–39

home renovations, 41–43, 51, 171, xvi
home seller self-assessment
   agent selection, 179–80
   buyer funnel, considering, 175–76
   contract-to-close period, 181–82
   curb appeal, 172–74
   interior, preparing, 173–74
   listing, developing, 177–78
   listing price, setting, 176–77
   location, assessing, 169–70
   negotiation, 180–81
   overview, 167
   pricing, determining, 168
   timing, choosing, 178–79
   value, increasing, 171
home warranties, 87–88
house design, effect on property value,
      34–36
housing market, identifying trends in. *See*
      market trends, identifying
Humphries, Stan, 96, 108, 110–11

I

iBuyers, 131–32
improvements, 25–26
income level, effect on property value, 29
Indoor airPLUS program, EPA, 44
initial listing price, anchoring, 145–46
inspections, home, 84–89, 158
interest-based bargaining, 155
interior of home
   buyer-requested repairs, 158–59,
      181–82
   cleaning, 70, 173–74
   color of paint, choosing, 65–66, 72
   data on staging, 70–72
   decluttering, 67–70, 173–74
   depersonalizing, 64–65
   home inspections, 84–89, 158
   home seller self-assessment of, 173–74
   renovations, 41–43, 51, 171, xvi
   staging suggestions, 72–73
investing in home renovations, 41–43, 51

J

job proximity, impact on property value,
      31–33
   just below strategy
   choosing, 99
   general discussion, 93–94
   home seller self-assessment of, 176–77
   research on, 95–96

K

kitchen remodels, 41–43
knowledge, role in negotiation, 137

L

land appreciates/buildings depreciate
      concept, 25–27
landscaping
   data on, 58–59
   general discussion, 57–58
   home seller self-assessment of, 172–73
   improving, 60
land value
   amenity proximity, impact on, 33–34
   job proximity, impact on, 31–33
   land appreciates/buildings depreciate
      concept, 25–27
   lot, impact on, 34–36
   neighborhood, impact on, 30–34
   region, impact on, 28–29
   school quality, impact on, 30–31
Leadership in Energy and Environmental
      Design (LEED) for Homes, 44
learned precision-magnitude association
      hypothesis, 97
leased solar panels, 49
length of listing description, 108
listings
   A/B testing, 102–3
   days on market, identifying market
      trends with, 142
   day to list, choosing, 119
   differentiators, highlighting for buyers,
      82–84
   examples of, 112–14

first 14 days, importance of, 120–21
home seller self-assessment of, 177–78
months of inventory, identifying market
    trends with, 142–43
ocular tracking, 102–3
optimal timing, choosing, 117–19
overview, 101
photos in, 104–7, 177–78
real estate agents, getting help from, 130
seasonal variations, 117–19
viewing pattern, 103–4
writing, 107–14
differentiators, including, 109–11
length of, 108
selection of words, 108–9
list price. *See also* pricing strategies
anchoring with, 145–46, 156
home seller self-assessment of, 168,
    176–77
list-price-to-close ratio, 143
loan assumption, 151
loan programs, government, 150–51
loans, bank, 150
local government policies, impact on prop-
    erty value, 29
location
    general discussion, 25–27
    home seller self-assessment of, 169–70
    of lot, impact on property value, 34–36
    neighborhood, effect on property value,
        30–34
    region, effect on property value, 28–29
losses versus gains, psychology of, 138–39
lot, impact on property value, 34–36, 170
low-end homes, listing descriptions for,
    109–11
low-price signal, 97

M

maintenance of homes, 26–27
marketing. *See also* listings
buyer risk, reducing, 84–89
day to list, choosing, 119
differentiators, highlighting for buyers,
    82–85
first 14 days, importance of, 120–21

optimal timing, choosing, 117–19
overview, 7
real estate agents, getting help from, 130
market price appreciation, 144–48
market trends, identifying
with days on market, 142
general discussion, 140–42
with list-price-to-close ratio, 143
with market price appreciation, 144–48
with months of inventory, 142–43
with number of showings, 143
submarkets, 141
mature trees, impact on property value,
    49–51
Meenan, Tim, 88
messy homes, impact on sales, 67–70
mid-tier homes, listing descriptions for,
    109–11
Miller, Jonathan, 31–32
MIT, study of agent value from, 128–29
months of inventory, identifying market
    trends with, 142–43
multiple listing service (MLS)
    green energy ratings, impact on value
        in, 47
    listings on, 7, 108
    real estate agents, value associated with,
        127–28, 129

N

National Association of Realtors, 129
negative words, in listing descriptions, 109
negotiation. *See also* market trends, identi-
    fying; options
anchor, establishing, 145–46, 156
basic concepts of, 137–39
in buyer funnel, 81–82
buyer-requested repairs, 158–59
conducting, 154–56
emotional requests in, 153
emotions, role in, 146–47
general discussion, 135–37
home seller self-assessment of, 180–81
initial listing price, effect on, 96
knowledge of other party, 144–45

mind-set of buyer and seller, understanding, 146–48
overview, 7
phases of process, 135–36, 139–42
psychology of gains versus losses,
138–39
real estate agents, getting help from, 130
reciprocity in, 155
research phase, 139–40
reservation price, 155–56
walkaway point, 137–38
neighborhood, effect on property value,
30–34, 169–70
neutral colors for interior, 65–66
New York, study on commute time and
property value in, 31–32
The New York Times, 31–32
Nova Scotia, value of cul-de-sac lots in, 36
number of showings, identifying market
trends with, 143

O

ocular tracking, 102–3
Offerpad, 131
offer phase, buyer funnel, 82
Old Dominion University, Virginia, study
on viewing patterns by, 103–4
online listings. *See also* writing listing
descriptions
A/B testing, 102–3
examples of, 112–14
ocular tracking, 102–3
overview, 101
photos in, 104–7
viewing pattern, 103–4
Opendoor, 131
open house, choosing date for, 118–19, 121
optimal timing, choosing, 117–19, 178–79
options
conditional sale clause, 152
due diligence, 152
earnest money payment, 152
financing, 150–51
other requests, 153–54
overview, 148–49
personal relationships, 154

timing, 149–50
outlier price scenarios, 20–24
overpricing, 14–15, 91

P

paint
exterior, 56–57, 61
interior, choosing, 65–66, 72
paired-data analysis, 8–9, 45–46
personal items, removing, 64–65, 173–74
personal relationships, options related to,
154
photos, in listings, 104–7, 177–78
photovoltaic (PV) cells, 47–49
pond analogy, 142–43
porch supports, updating, 56, 60–61
power washing, 61
precise pricing strategy
choosing, 99
general discussion, 94
home seller self-assessment of, 176–77
research on, 95–98
Priceonomics, 24
pricing. *See also* automated valuation models; pricing strategies
amenity proximity, impact on, 33–34
anchor price, establishing, 145–46, 156
baseline, establishing, 18–24
buyer funnel, research phase in, 80
curb appeal, impact on, 58–59
data analytics, increasing with, 2–6
5 to 10 percent sales price increase, 4–6,
24
general discussion, 13–15
hedonic regression, 8, 9
home seller self-assessment of, 168
job proximity, impact on, 31–33
listing description, impact of, 109–11
market appreciation, identifying market
trends with, 144
overpricing, 14, 91
paired-data analysis, 8–9
professional versus amateur photos,
impact of, 105–7
school quality, impact on, 30–31
pricing strategies

home seller self-assessment of, 176–77
just below, 93–94, 95–96, 99
precise, 94, 95–98, 99
research on, 95–99
round number, 92–93, 95–96, 99
probable selling price, 21
product, viewing home as, 11–12
professional versus amateur photos, 105–7
property disclosure forms, 84–89
property value. *See* value
psychological pricing, 93
psychology of gains versus losses, 138–39
PV (photovoltaic) cells, 47–49

Q

questions to ask real estate agents, 130
quick sales, 22, 71–72

R

Rascoff, Spencer, 17, 96, 108, 110–11
real estate agents
    best practices for, xvii–xviii
    commissions, 125, 127, 128–29
    governmental control on, 124
    home seller assessment of, 179–80
    iBuyer services as alternative to, 131–32
    pricing process, 15
    questions to ask, 130
    real value of, 129–31
    reasons for hiring, 129–31
    selecting, 6–7, 123
    skills of, 124–25
    value of, research on, 126–29
real estate investors, xviii–xix
Real Estate Staging Association, 72
reciprocity in negotiation, 155
Redfin
    accuracy of estimates, 17
    AVMs used by, 15–18
    big-data approach, 9–10
    iBuyer services, 131–32
    professional versus amateur photos,
        impact of, 105
    walkability, impact on property value, 34
regional demographics, 28

region, impact on property value, 28–29,
    169
regression analysis, 46
remodeling, 41–43, 51, 171, xvi
Remodeling magazine, 42
renovations, 41–43, 51, 171, xvi
repairs, buyer-requested, 158–59, 181–82
research
    buyer funnel phase, 80
    before negotiation, 139–40. *See also* mar-
        ket trends, identifying
    on pricing strategies, 95–99
reservation price, 155–56, 180–81
Residential Energy Services Network
    (RESNET), 45
risk, reducing, 84–89
round number strategy
choosing, 99
general discussion, 92–93
home seller self-assessment of, 176–77
research on, 95–96

S

sales preparation
    cleaning, 70
    data on staging, 70–72
    decluttering, 67–70
    depersonalizing, 64–65
    overview, 7, 63
    paint colors, choosing, 65–66
    suggestions for, 72–73
sales price
    baseline, establishing, 18–24
    distribution of potential selling prices,
        23–24
    factors affecting range of, 20–22
    5 to 10 percent increase on, 4–6, 24
    general discussion, 13–15
    hedonic regression, 8, 9
    home seller self-assessment of, 168
    list-price-to-close ratio, identifying
        market trends with, 143
    market appreciation, identifying market
        trends with, 144
    outlier price scenarios, 20–23
    paired-data analysis, 8–9

reasons for high, 22–23
reasons for low, 22–23
time on market, impact on, 120–21
school quality, impact on property value,
    30–31
seasonal variations in markets, 117–19,
    178–79
Seattle, Washington, study on commute
    time and property value in, 32–33
Seiler, Michael, 95
self-assessment for home seller. *See* home
    seller self-assessment
seller financing, 151
seller's market, identifying
    with days on market, 142
    general discussion, 140–42
    with list-price-to-close ratio, 143
    with market price appreciation, 144–48
    with months of inventory, 142–43
    with number of showings, 143
    submarkets, 141
shortlist phase, buyer funnel, 80
showings
    market trends, identifying with number
        of, 143
    open house, choosing date for, 118–19,
        121
    visiting phase, in buyer funnel, 81
siding, 56–57, 61
signing contracts, 157
size of houses, 34–35, 108–9
skills of real estate agents, 124–25
small homes, words associated with, 108
solar panels, 47–49
square footage, 34–35
staging
    cleaning, 70
    data on, 70–72
    decluttering, 67–70
    depersonalizing, 64–65
    home seller self-assessment of, 173–74
    minimal, 73
    overview, 63
    paint colors, choosing, 65–66
    suggestions for, 72–73
Stanford University, study of agent value
    from, 127–28

strategies for pricing. *See* pricing strategies
stress hormones, effect of messy homes on,
    68–69
subsidies for solar panels, 48
summer months, home sales during, 118
surveys, 84–89
syllables in sales price, 99

T

Texas A&M University, study of agent value
    by, 127–28
Texas Tech University, study on curb appeal
    by, 58
time on market, impact on sales price,
    120–21
timing
    day to list, choosing, 119
    first 14 days, importance of, 120–21
    home seller self-assessment of, 178–79
    of offer, 149–50
    seasonal variations, 117–19
topography, effect on property value, 28–29
transportation proximity, effect on property
    value, 29
trees, impact on property value, 49–51
Trulia
    accuracy of estimates, 17
    AVMs used by, 15–18
    big-data approach, 9–10

U

University of Chicago, study on agent value
    by, 126
University of Washington, study on tree
    value by, 50
university towns, home sale cycle in, 118
US Department of Veterans Affairs (VA)
    loans, 150–51
US Environmental Protection Agency
    (EPA) ratings, 44
utility, 7

V

vacation destinations, home sales in, 118
value. *See also* automated valuation models;
    differentiators, highlighting
    amenity proximity, impact on, 33–34
    appraisers, role of, 36–39
    baseline, establishing, 18–24
    data analytics, 2–6
    data, creating with, 6–10
    5 to 10 percent sales price increase, 4–6,
      24
    general discussion, 13–15
    hedonic regression, 8, 9
    home renovations, increasing with,
      41–43, 51
    home seller self-assessment of, 171
    house design, impact on, 34–36
    job proximity, impact on, 31–33
    land appreciates/buildings depreciate
      concept, 25–27
    lot, impact on, 34–36
    neighborhood, impact on, 30–34
    paired-data analysis, 8–9
    real estate agents, getting help from, 130
    region, impact on, 28–29
    school quality, impact on, 30–31
    specific house prices, estimating, 40
    trees, impact on, 49–51
value of real estate agents, 126–29
VA (US Department of Veterans Affairs)
    loans, 150–51
viewing pattern, 103–4
vinyl window replacements, 41–43
visiting phase, buyer funnel, 81

W

walkability, impact on property value,
    33–34
walkaway point, 137–38
Walk Score, 33–34
warranties, home, 87–88
Washington, DC, green premium in, 46
WaterSense program, EPA, 44
windows
    cleaning, 61
    replacing, 41–43

winter months, home sales during, 117–18
writing listing descriptions, 107–14
    differentiators, including, 109–11
    examples of, 112–14
    home seller self-assessment of, 177–78
    length of, 108
    selection of words, 108–9

Y

yard, 57–58

Z

zeros, in sales prices, 97–98
Zillow
    accuracy of estimates, 17
    AVMs used by, 15–18
    big-data approach, 9–10
    iBuyer services, 131–32
    interest in homes after listing, 120–21
    optimal timing, choosing, 118–19
    pricing strategy analysis, 96
    study on impact of colors, 66
    walkability, impact on value, 34
Zillow Talk (Humphries and Rascoff), 96,
    108, 110–11
zoning policies, effect on property value, 29

ABOUT THE
AUTHOR

Jack Richards is the founder of Integere LLC, a boutique consulting firm with deep expertise in converting data into practical actions to improve the financial performance of organizations. Jack has nearly two decades of experience leading and advising large organizations with a focus on achieving tangible results. He is passionate about the buying and selling of real estate and is a licensed real estate agent and REALTOR® in North Carolina. Jack is a graduate of the Tuck School of Business at Dartmouth College and the University of Virginia. He also served in the US Army. Jack lives in North Carolina with his wife, Kristen, and their young daughter.